Q

Snippets from a Rideshare Driver

R.C. OTOVIC

Published by Richter Publishing LLC www.richterpublishing.com

Editors: Margarita Martinez, Monica San Nicolas & Marisa Holste-Beetz

Cover Design: Brianna Lopez

ISBN-10:1945812524
ISBN-13:9781945812521

DISCLAIMER

This book is designed to provide information on rideshare only. This information is provided and sold with the knowledge that the publisher and author do not offer any legal or medical advice. In the case of a need for any such expertise, consult with the appropriate professional. This book does not contain all information available on the subject. This book has not been created to be specific to any individual's or organization's situation or needs. Every effort has been made to make this book as accurate as possible. However, there may be typographical and/ or content errors. Therefore, this book should serve only as a general guide and not as the ultimate source of subject information. This book contains information that might be dated and is intended only to educate and entertain. The author and publisher shall have no liability or responsibility to any person or entity regarding any loss or damage incurred, or alleged to have incurred, directly or indirectly, by the information contained in this book. You hereby agree to be bound by this disclaimer or you may return this book within the guarantee time period for a full refund. In the interest of full disclosure, this book contains affiliate links that might pay the author or publisher a commission upon any purchase from the company. While the author and publisher take no responsibility for the business practices of these companies and or the performance of any product or service, the author or publisher has used the product or service and makes a recommendation in good faith based on that experience. All characters appearing in this work are fictitious. Any resemblance to real persons, living or dead, is purely coincidental.

DEDICATION

This book is dedicated to two women who meant more than life to me.

Nancy Kimball Kent Otovic
February 18, 1926 to September 12, 2011

Dorothy Howell Dettner
May 2, 1915 to January 10, 1988

CONTENTS

ACKNOWLEDGMENTS

To Colby, Drew, Jasmin and Ariyana, I hope you grow up to do whatever it is you want to do in life and are as happy and successful as possible.

Bob and Nancy Otovic, thank you for the support I have received all through the years.

To represent the Otovic family name is a tremendous honor. To all my aunts and uncles who showed me how, thank you.

Thank you for the great photos from Norma at Normabringuier.com and a special thanks to my Salem brother Michael Fritz for beta reading and giving me full feedback and advice on my original manuscript.

To Michael Essex for his awesome marketing skills and for asking me every free second of his time how things were coming along.

Thank you to my good friend Ryan Wood for the laughter and brotherhood while in the Q.

Thanks to the Boston sports scene for the last 25 years and congratulations to the teams on their successes and accomplishments.

I thank Kim, a thousand times over, for putting up with me while I worked on this project from researching and writing to seeing it come to reality and helping me market it. She is the most positive person I have ever met in my life and she means the world to me.

This book was written for all the people in the world who enjoy a good laugh and can understand a joke. And if you can't, whateva.

INTRODUCTION

Q. \ 'kyü \ *A line or sequence of people or vehicles awaiting their turn to be attended to or to proceed or a list of data items, commands, etc., stored so as to be retrievable in a definite order, usually the order of insertion.*

When C.D. Howell left his job in the spring of 2017 to become a full-time rideshare driver, he never imagined the types of personalities his riders would have or how easy it would be for them to open up and submerge him into their most private, intimate stories.

Insane, captivating pure humor, but on the proverbial sick side.

Howell invites you into his car, into the Q at Tampa International Airport. Listen as he types the stories into his cell phone with two thumbs while he waits and hangs with the members of his inner circle in the cell lot. They play cards and smoke cigarettes, watch planes fly overhead, and wait for you, the airplane passenger, to call and have them take you to their destination.

Grab a coffee, light up a smoke, and raise your hand as they share stories about riders and their troubles in their daily lives, gross subjects, and taste-test your food deliveries before arrival. Learn about their difficulties in getting gas, dealing with debit and credit machine issues, and shaking hands with a rider while wondering, *did they really wash their hands after they peed?*

Listen to him explain a simple science and his keys to making money. Thirty different stories will touch all of your emotions as you think, cry, and laugh hysterically.

Later, through C.D.'s eyes, learn from his experience in the transportation business for over 25 years about how he would attempt to repair ridesharing.

It's sweeping the world as a very popular means of affordable transportation. This is the other side of airport rideshare travel, the side you never thought existed. He has more than a minute to explain.

We have entered at number 130.

Welcome into the Q.

THE Q

Okay, I can't hide this fact from you readers any longer, yet I feel zero guilt in my disclosure. My name is C.D. Howell and I'm a rideshare driver.

There, I said it; like a confession under the lights of an interrogation room while at police central.

For those of you who don't know, a rideshare driver shares his car to escort people who need a ride to their destination.

I stand 6'6" tall and weigh about 330 lbs., sporting long, flowing brown hair and a full-grown beard. Some say my size equates to an NFL offensive lineman or, even better, I've been told lately, a Viking.

I'm originally from a small town outside Boston, Massachusetts. For the last ten years, I've lived in Tampa, FL, with my girlfriend Ava, her daughter, Rosa, and my two boys, Alexander and Josh. These days, I spend most of my time sitting in the parking lot at Tampa International Airport, or what we commonly refer to as the Queue.

While I'm in the Q, I wait in a slate-gray 2016 Toyota Corolla. It has four doors, which is a requirement for ridesharing, a cloth interior, and a strong enough A/C system to make your nipples freeze in a short amount of time. Being in Florida, that is a major perk. Pun intended.

Queue, \ ˈkyü \ *a line or sequence of people or vehicles awaiting their turn to be attended to or to proceed or a list of data items, commands, etc., stored so as to be retrievable in a definite order, usually the order of insertion.*

Our Queue at the airport issues a virtual number when you enter the

3

vicinity of the cell parking lot, much like pulling a ticket at the deli counter in the grocery store. I'm waiting for number one so I can be called for a ride. I update my phone periodically to see what number I am, although I'm not waiting to order a half pound of roast beef and a quarter pound of baby Swiss cheese, sliced extremely thin. I love sandwiches, btw. I always order my sandwiches covered in tomato, onions and mayo, sprinkles of black pepper, and occasionally jalapenos. Yummy. And now, after living down here for a while, the thought of a pressed sandwich with the garlic mayo they put on them, wow! It's hard to find the good bread down here, though; the bread is much better up in the northeast. OH, and cut it in half please, diagonally. I like it that way.

Sorry! I run off on tangents from now to then. I could talk about sandwiches for hours.

Morning, noon, or at night, whatever shift I choose to work, I sit and wait for my number to be called. I'm in the queue waiting to pick you up. Leave the vicinity of the lot and your Q number resets. Shut your phone off to reset it, it sticks, or you shut off an app by accident, and well, you lose. Back to the end of the line.

You're landing soon. We can see the planes flying over our heads, and I'll eventually be called to pick you up. At any time of the day, hundreds of drivers filter through the cell phone parking lot, looking for a queue number and a ride. Cars zoom around the lot like the inside of a bumper car track, but not looking to crash, thankfully. On a good day, a driver will pass through the lot about 10-12 times. Their purpose is to drive you, the airline passenger, to your residence or to a hotel where you may be vacationing or on business, or anywhere else you need to go.

To be kind, I'll ask you certain questions during our ride: how your flight was, where you came in from. Then I'll travel roads, in good or bad weather, to get you safely to your destination. I do this full-time. Yet, people ask, and some have even said, really?

To myself and the inner circle of drivers that I spend time with in the Q, a regular job sucks. Been there, done that. I took time off during 2017 because I was highly burned out from the corporate world. Too many bosses telling me what to do, following orders, and exhausting my time on the regular minutiae that people dislike about their jobs. I also wanted to have more flexibility to spend with my two boys, ages 16 and 11, going to water parks during the summer, attending doctor's appointments, and cheering them on at their basketball games—the stuff that most parents say is pretty important to them, yet many people work through their children's lives and don't blink an eye. They miss so much stuff that they never really get a chance to know who their children turn into.

I've been in the transportation business for the last 25 years, mostly delivery driving. I've transported dangerous goods, hazmat materials, and regular packages. Now, I've decided to try transporting people. If I have a coffee with me, I can drive just about anywhere and do anything. The transfer of my life to Florida has not stopped my love of hot coffee. I get downright irritated when I pull up to order coffee and the drive-thru clerk says, "You mean hot coffee?"

Is there any other fucking way to drink coffee? It's brewed hot, right? Then give it here. I mean, I'm not going to sit here and rag on half of Florida for drinking fufu cold or frozen coffee drinks, but just because it's 100 degrees out, why am I looked upon like I'm crazy for ordering a hot cup of coffee?

Enough said. I don't need cream or sugar; I'll drink hot coffee however I can get it. I like Irish cream, if I can have my way. Hey, I'm from Beantown.

I'm an enormous sports fan. Being from Boston, it's pretty much a requirement, given the recent success of the teams over the last 20 years. People call me passionate when I discuss major sports. Northeast people are usually labeled as blue-collar, hardworking people who pay attention very well and we don't accept mediocracy. We also have the same commitment to our sports programs.

It's easy to talk about sports in the car with a stranger because most men follow sports, and most women roll their eyes at their men who follow sports, so it can be a common bond to strike up a conversation. Also, everyone has an opinion, and most people can't be wrong because that's who they watch and cheer for. Who am I to tell them they're full of shit?

Nonetheless, I support my teams in sticker form on the trunk of my car: Celtics, Red Sox, and Patriots. That usually spikes a conversation or two, or, like I call it, passionate discussion.

Keeping customers is the goal, since I'm ranked upon performance. Currently, I'm ranked the highest out of my group of airport friends. One woman commented on my personal information board that I'm "an absolute Boston legend." Bird, Orr, Brady, Ortiz, C.D.—that puts me in an elite category.

I've given over 1,600 rides and have over 900 5-star ratings. That equals up to a 4.96 out of 5.00-star rating.

Believe me, people really look at those ratings. I once had a woman tell me she will never get into a car with any driver below a 4.95, so I guess I just qualified. She said she literally cancels rides with any driver who falls below her criteria. At the start of all of this, I never knew ratings meant so much. I just treat people how I want to be treated.

Seriously, without customers, I couldn't tell you readers all this juicy shit.

Most of my stories are written very quickly in my cell phone notes app right after they've happened. Sitting in the Q, waiting for my number to be called, I pound away on my phone with two thumbs, then transfer all the notes to my laptop. One day, Ms. Ava and I sat down and she told me that I really had a good base for a book, which I'd kind of always wanted to write.

I don't just enjoy writing as a hobby; I have a journalism education. During time served at two major journalism universities, I held editorial positions and wrote my own column.

My penname, "I Otto Know," is a long story. I can only say thank you to my good friend Parry for issuing that title.

It's funny, and unexpected, how honest people get when they have some time in a car to just sit back and open up about their lives. I guess you have a lot of time during a 20-30-minute drive, staring out the window and listening to the radio. Some people open up fast, and others take a little talking at first, but gosh, have I heard some stories. Make no mistake about it; I'm not a writer with a wild imagination. I'm a bored ex-journalism major with extra time on his hands who finds telling hysterical stories therapeutic, as well as making people laugh. I have a quirky sense of humor and find odd shit funny.

I'm the guy who enjoys getting a coffee, on Black Friday, of course, traveling to a store at the perfect time the special deal is about to roll out and watching two women trying to violently beat each other senseless to obtain the last $99 blue light special TV. I'm sure I'm not the only one.

I also giggled hardcore when hearing that, during our recent hurricane prep, two men tried to punch each other out trying to buy the last piece of plywood. Six days before the storm was set to arrive, I'd have been the guy in the back, yelling, "Hit him in the face! Get that board!" More on that later, in Chapter 26, "Level 42."

My beautiful girlfriend Ava always says I can get on a roll and that it's hard for her to get a word in. There are also times where I'm very quiet, and those are the moments where I'm watching and soaking in the things around me. I love laughter; sometimes, unfortunately, at other people's expense. Even so, very few people can make me laugh out loud. That doesn't mean I'm not cracking up inside.

All of these experiences you're about to read are based on true events with true people. Names, of course, have been changed to protect the innocent—although, during my time driving, I've told people, on occasion, that I want to write a book. Once, I had an author in the car. First thing she told me was change everyone's names, no matter how close you all are to each other.

Riders have asked what the book will be called and "can I do something crazy to be in it?"

Some people don't wait to find out anything about me writing a book; they're just naturally crazy.

Like Frank and Dan, who qualify right up there with the best of them.

Frank was from NY and Dan was from Chicago. They arrived in Florida in March to see a baseball spring training game. They were out in front of a huge building downtown, waiting for a ride, and I couldn't find them. I'd driven around the thing twice.

It was Sunday, about 11:25 a.m., and all of a sudden, my phone rang.

"Is this C.D.?" the voice said.

"Yes."

"Umm, okay, so do you have a gray car?" the voice asked.

"Yes," I repeated.

"Toyota Corolla?"

"Right again," I said.

"Do you have a fuckin' piece of shit Red Sox sticker on the back of it?"

I smirked; that must be a New Yorker.

"Hold on, I'll turn around," I said. "Where are you?"

"Hold on, stay right frigging there," the voice said. "We're running up behind you."

A tall skinny man entered the back on the car on the passenger's side while a shorter husky guy got in behind my seat, and both car doors slammed.

"I'm from New York," the taller man described. "I knew that Red Sox sticker sucks comment would get ya," he said, laughing hard.

"I'm from Chicago," the other man said. "We aren't like that."

"Because you are fucking losers, too," Frank said, laughing.

Later in the ride, Frank asked me if we could stop and get some smokes and a few beers at any local pharmacy or gas station.

"Oh yeah, and suntan lotion, too," Dan said. "We need that."

"No, it's not fucking lotion, it's sunscreen," Frank said. "Damn, you make us sound like lovers if you call it lotion. I won't ever share lotion with you, even if you are my best friend. Damn it, you make us sound like a couple of lovers when you say it like that."

"Lotion, screen, oil, it's all the same shit, peckerhead," Dan replied.

"The fuck it is," Frank says. "We ain't sharing no lotion, okay? That's it, that's all, that's the end of it."

As I pulled up in front of the grocery store, just before the stadium, I told the boys this was the best option for getting all of their needs.

"So, this has your beers, smokes, food, skin protection products," I smirked and raised my eyebrows.

"Cool. I'll go," Dan says.

"No, no, no. No, you won't," Frank retorted. "I'll end up with the wrong cigarettes and wine coolers. Oh, and lotion. I'll go. You stay here."

"Fucking hate wine coolers, and what did I do?" Dan looked at me like I'd known him for 20 years.

"C.D., do you need nothing?" Frank asked.

"I'm good. Thanks for asking, though," I responded.

I do have some crazy stories, and I've seen some funny stuff. My stories aren't about nudity, perverse acts in the car, or anything of that nature. I'm not a rock band bus driver—although, coincidentally, I had one of those in my car once. Great guy from Valrico, FL. We shared stories. I got to see the nudity and craziness of the rock band side, literally. The man had more naked women pictures on his phone than a nude magazine.

I wasn't surprised at all.

9

But in the end, I had him laughing at my stories. Just pure humor, but on the proverbial sick side.

Class participation will be required during your time reading these stories. You will be frequently asked to please raise your right hand when and if my experiences have happened to you. If I have done my best and written well, everybody will raise their hand at least once.

I'm sure many of you reading this have used ridesharing at one time or another. It's sweeping the world as a very popular means of affordable transportation. This is the other side of airport rideshare travel, the side you never thought existed. I have more than a minute.

We've entered at number 130.

Welcome into the Q.

THE BOARD AND SIMPLE SCIENCE

My friends and I drive around in our own cars, listen to people's stories, and get paid. No boss, no deadlines. We get to be on vacation with people. If only for a few minutes, we're living through their lives, like part-time travel agents. We drive them around and explain where to go to keep busy, have a good time, or have a great dinner. And most of us who do this full-time for a living make decent money. But I will admit, there is a science in where you go and what you do. Our moves are predominantly calculated.

Hotels and airports play a big part of business for me, so I concentrate on getting my rides from there. The airport is especially busy with riders in the morning. Some are professionals on business trips, but most are vacationers, either arriving for one or coming home from one.

Checkout time for most hotels is 10-11 a.m. So, if I'm floating around a block of hotels at that time, I'm probably guaranteed to get a ride to the airport and back into the queue.

Why is my choice of rides concentrated to and from the airport? All science.

The airport equals safety for Ava and me; we decided this after talking about this profession a lot. TSA prescreens travelers going into an airport gate. You are hopefully not getting past any level of security with a gun or a knife on you, so there's less chance of anyone carrying weapons while I transport them. Also, I once had an airline employee tell me that if airport security even suspects that you're drunk, you won't be able to pass security, let alone board a plane. So, I've eliminated weapons and drunks from my car. I don't want to be driving around shit-faced pedestrians at 2:00 a.m., after they get out of a bar. I don't have time for that shit in my life. My old man used to say, if you're in a situation that could carry a problem, maybe you shouldn't have put yourself in a situation that could pose a problem. Sounds logical.

It's Tuesday morning at 6:15 a.m. 82 degrees. 10 mph NW winds.

Planes are coming in toward the airport through the sunrise off the bay to land over us. We can see the day unfolding in the air before you even touch the ground.

"I can't believe it's this high; too many people are here. How are we supposed to make any money?" says Jax, shaking his head while staring at the electronic flight board in the middle of the cell lot.

Jax is an ex vet, probably around 57, although I've never asked. He runs about 6', 190 lbs., and I've never seen him without a white golf hat on. He's a part-time real estate agent, retired, and does rideshares for extra money.

"Just too damn many. And all I'm going to get is a $7 ride to downtown, carry heavy bags, and not get a tip."

An honest, hardworking guy, Jax is a good friend of mine and hates not getting tipped, especially when he handles bags. The day is coming when he'll blow up, and look out when it happens. We've always said in the inner circle that he'll eventually snap, flip his lid, and be the second coming of Defcon 5. Jax's opinions are usually well-articulated and logical. But he has a personality where detailed, meaningless shit drives him crazy.

He's now number 47 in the Queue.

"You look too fucking rich," Mathieu tells Jax. "You look too nice—nice car, nice clothes—people aren't going to tip your ass. That's your problem."

Standing at about 6'3", 385 lbs., Mathieu played offensive line for a major West Coast university and has more college degrees than you can count with a calculator. Mathieu is also a former litigation attorney who quit his firm to do this.

Yes, this.

His husband has a federal job that meets their monthly bill requirements, so Mathieu does this for play money. He does this because we all genuinely love what we do. He takes pride in wearing his $3 discount shirts and shorts, more for his comfort than the look, but you wouldn't know it. Yet he drives a 2017 Toyota Camry and his hubby drives a 2017 SUV. The tip jar at the front of his car, considered a coffee cup holder by most, is full of singles and $5 bills. Completely full.

Mathieu is full of laughter and wit. He's one of the few people I've hung around with in my life who waits for me to speak, then pauses for a second to deliver their choice of punchline. Sarcastic tones are what mostly come out of his mouth. If a member of the group bums a cigarette and a light in the group, he's quick to comment.

"Man, you left the house today without all your important essentials. I don't have any children for a reason; I'm not into supporting you." Then he always hands over a cigarette. He's a very generous, caring person, but he's always going to let you know you're a needy bitch.

With that being said, Mathieu and I enjoy and understand the delivery of a good joke. He has told me thousands of times that we were born with the same purpose in life.

"You know I love you, right?" he said to me in the car one day as we waited for rides.

I stared at him. "Really?"

"Well, not like that, and you wish, because you couldn't handle all of this. But I love your humor and the fact that you can be a dick sometimes and deliver the best comebacks. I just love it!" he said as he clapped his hands and leaned toward the steering wheel.

"Oh, God!" he screamed.

He loves to get excited for small reasons.

After delivering a comeback to something someone says, we frequently beep our car horns to punctuate the joke. We get plenty of stares from other drivers in the lot, but fuck them if they can't take a joke.

God bless Mathieu. We get each other.

"I look like a bum—ripped shirt—so I get tips," Mathieu continues. "Got $20 from a ride this morning. So there."

"You get tips because you use good lube," Branson retorts, walking out of the bathroom and heading to his car. "Admit it!"

"Shhh, you're not supposed to give that information away," Mathieu laughs.

"Honey, your information isn't a secret, no matter who you think you're kidding," Branson fires back.

God knows if he's serious or not and I don't have any interest in finding out. I mean less than zero.

Branson is a small man, about 5'3", a frail figure, and is usually identified very easily by the purple wool painter's cap that he wears daily and his thick black-rimmed glasses. He's usually dressed in blue jeans and has a wide variety of plaid shirts. He's dated half of the men in the greater Tampa area, yet we usually hear about the war stories with him and his ex, Jeremiah. They broke up a while ago now, but still live in the same apartment and both rideshare, so it's difficult to not see them in the same vicinity, talking and sometimes arguing.

Branson's a lifer at the lot. He's tried many other jobs and eventually tells his bosses to go piss off, so then he ends up back here. Because of his frequent short rides out of the lot, Branson is referred to by most as "Q3." The shortest ride you can tally for ridesharing is usually between $3 or $4 and the Q, in this case, stands for queen. People with the shortest rides of the day are usually called K3 or Q3 for the day.

Branson is also the lot's fashion police. If you aren't supposed to be wearing those shoes with that shirt or your hair is a mess, it can be similar to watching a red-carpet show while he sits and stares and smokes a 100 cigarette as he critiques other drivers in a subtle high-pitched voice.

About 10 of us meet in the cell lot every morning to get in the Queue. Usually our cars are backed into the spots, neatly lined toward the board. Restrooms are in the center of the lot. There are garbage cans everywhere, even though a lot of trash blows around in the wind.

What more could we want out of life?

We have a soda and snack machine located near the bathrooms, and from time to time, Mr. Guido's lunch wagon pulls in and parks from about 10:30 in the morning to 4:00 or 5:00 in the afternoon.

It's the most ordinary $11 hamburger I've ever had. Shitty cheese, too.

"At least they could put more pepper on the bitch," Branson says.

This is our office, where we come to work daily. Most people hang around the water cooler and talk about something they saw on TV last night; we have our parking lot.

The yellow electronic digital flight board over in the front left of the lot shows arrival and departure times and city origin. It gives us an estimate of how long we'll be waiting for you. Groans and ahhhs can be heard from time to time as the board updates. Delays and early arrivals change constantly, especially with the sudden weather in Tampa Bay.

The airport estimates that 18-20 people per flight will use rideshare services and then you have to add 25 minutes from when they land for people to get luggage and arrive curbside. As soon as a rider calls, number one in the Queue gets a ping on their app and everyone remaining moves up a spot. Customers are told not to call for a ride until they enter the baggage claim area just inside the terminal curbside pickup area. For one thing, airport services take time to unload bags and then transport them to the belts that spurt them out to awaiting passengers. However, many people call the second the plane lands, which can have us pulling through terminals, circling around, and looking for your ass that can't follow a simple set of directions.

Time is money. Drivers don't want to be circling an area at eight cents a minute. They want to find you, pick you up, and get you on your way so they can flip you into another ride.

Howard pulls in. Brand-new black Toyota Camry, nicely shined. He takes a lot of pride in it and wipes his car down constantly.

"I'm 141. WTF? Time to clean my tires with this new shining solution I bought."

Howard is also known for wearing black tank tops and reading glasses. He can't see shit. He's one of those people who isn't ashamed to wear multiple pairs of reading glasses if he has to put them on top of each other to see small print.

"Pittsburgh and Ft. Lauderdale are the first flights. They're landing at 7:25 and 7:32," says Jax. "I don't want that local shit. Too close."

Drivers love to drive longer distances in the morning. They're fresh from resting and miles mean money. Short-distance flights are usually filled with Florida business travelers who may just be going to a local hotel or to sign a deal, show a house, or do some other sort of business.

Justin drives through the gate and pulls up next to my car in his Nissan Altima.

"I brought donuts, but only coffee for me. What the fuck? Is this right? I'm at 150," he says with an irritated look on his face.

Justin will have a bit of a wait, so it's good he brought donuts to keep himself occupied. He stands about 6' tall and a good stiff tailwind from a plane coming in from the south would blow him over. He's not frail by any means, but he's very skinny. As far as overall good guys, Justin is at the top of the list. He and I are probably the closest friends at the lot. We hang out in our free time, although not a lot, because we live a decent distance from each other and both have two children, but I do enjoy Justin's wit, sports knowledge, and conversation. We can strike up a conversation about anything in the world. Like myself, Justin's a huge baseball and football fan, so, while flicking butts, we usually rap about your poor running-back scenario or how an umpire missed a call last night.

Cigarette smoke blows wildly through the driver huddle as they stand by one driver's car, telling war stories, playing cards, or catching up with friends they haven't seen in a while. Many drink their coffee or, in Mathieu's case, eat. He's always eating. You'll understand what I mean later on.

"So, I had a few drunks in my car last night," Branson says. "I thought one was going to puke in my car just before it ended. So, I was like, honey, get the hell out of here, boys. No need for that."

"One puked in my car last week," a guy walking by our group says.

"Who's that fuckin' guy?" Mathieu asks, looking at me with a puzzled look on his face.

Groups at the lot are usually pretty tight. Individuals don't usually hang out with other groups unless they receive an invite.

"I don't know. Did someone say they brought donuts?" I asked.

I love donuts. Any kind of donuts. They go with coffee. Circles, sticks, hell, even the little balls that look like they're the missing circular sphere that fell out of a regular donut, I love them.

Raise your hand if you like donuts. I'll give you an easy one for your first one.

We all have a bit of a wait today, but nice weather, donuts, smokes, coffee, good friendships, and telling a few stories should keep us occupied. Are you ready?

I'm now number 118.

THE YELLOW HOTEL

I can be at a disadvantage in this world when someone doesn't speak English. I've always been told I talk funny because of my accent, yet at times I can have tremendous difficultly understanding thick accents. As a result, I often find myself staring at a person's mouth while they're talking, trying to make out what they're saying.

Trying to get people to their destination is usually pretty easy, though, because the address appears on my phone. It's pretty simple if it's already entered, and the app shows the origin of your destination and address. Right?

Should be. But isn't always.

Isabella entered my car one gloomy Thursday and spoke very little English. I picked her up from the red terminal and all she really said was "hi" when she got in. I asked her if she was going downtown and she nodded while looking through her purse, not paying attention to me, so I pulled out and carried on.

She was speaking with a thick Spanish accent. I managed many Puerto Rican workers during my years of truck driving.

I can't speak Spanish.

Yes, I know I live in Tampa.

Yes, I understand that most people in the Tampa area speak very good español.

Yes, I do live very close to Cuba, Puerto Rico, and Mexico.

I can't speak Spanish, okay? I'm not going to turn anything into a political debate, but I do believe I'm one of the few who thinks that if you live in a country, you should learn to speak the country's language and be able to communicate with the locals.

Raise your hands if you're with me, brothers and sisters.

Now, I do hope my book *Q* is printed in many different languages in the future, so all people can read and enjoy it. But right then, Isabella and I were going to have a rough ride.

The app said Hilton Hotel, downtown district, so off we went down I-275 North. Because we couldn't relate to each other at all, the car ride was very quiet until we pulled up to the Hilton. Now, I once drove a man to Sarasota, almost an hour away from the airport. He spoke broken English—really broken—and fluent Spanish. But by the time I got to Sarasota, I understood how much he valued his rojo Chevy truck. No such conversation with Isabella.

The hotel was about where business picked up, as an old friend of mine used to say.

One word Isabella could say very well in English was "yellow." So when we pulled up in front of the all-blue/black glass window-covered Hilton, I was very surprised.

"Okay, here we go," I said, noting that we'd arrived at her destination.

"No," she screamed. "Yellow!"

Yellow??

I'm like, *okay, what does yellow mean? This hotel is surrounded by glass windows. There's not a speck of yellow coloring anywhere around.* But she said it with conviction, so something was wrong.

As I popped the trunk to get her bag, I noticed she wasn't moving. She wouldn't get out. What could I do?

"Okay, so you're saying the hotel is yellow?" I put her bag back in the trunk and shut it.

"Yellow," she said, nodding her head. She was one hundred percent convinced we were at the wrong place. I was one hundred percent sure we were at the right place, but she wasn't budging.

Where the fuck could I find a yellow hotel?

I got my phone and used an online translator. At this point, it was all I had to communicate with this woman.

Okay, translate. "Are you going to a hotel that is yellow?"

She read it.

"Yellow," she said, nodding her head fast. Suddenly, she couldn't speak Spanish or English, just yellow.

Okay ... let's go find a yellow hotel. I didn't have the faintest clue as to where, but whatever.

I drove this woman around in my car for almost 90 minutes, through what felt like all of the streets of Tampa.

Radisson? Nope.

DoubleTree? Nope.

Marriott? Nope.

Comfort Suites? Nope.

Hyatt? Nope.

La Quinta? Nope.

Holiday Inn? Nope.

Grrrrrr. Can you imagine doing that for someone you like, never mind someone you don't even know?

Raise your hand if you would have tried to throw her out of the car a long time ago.

Finally, I asked her with my phone, "So, do you have a phone number of somebody at the hotel we can call?"

"Yes, but my phone doesn't work here. It only works in Columbia," she replied through text translate.

WTF?

"Okay, so I have a phone, and it works just fine in the USA. Gimme the number."

She gave me the number of her brother, José, who was staying at the hotel she wanted to go to. I dialed the number and a man answered. I put him on Bluetooth so we could both hear him in the car and the woman started quickly speaking in Spanish.

"Hold on," I yelled at her. I was putting a fucking end to this shit. I didn't have any more patience. "José, do you speak English?"

"Very well," he answers.

"Great. I have your sister Isabella in the car. What hotel are you staying at?"

"The Hilton, downtown," he replied.

"I thought so," I said. "Do me a favor? I'll be there in about 10 minutes. Please walk down to the lobby and wait for us outside. She doesn't seem to want to get out of the car. I guess she doesn't like that hotel or doesn't think you're inside it."

"Okay, no problem," he laughed. "That's my sister."

Well, your sister is a pain in the ass.

About 15 minutes later, as we pulled up in front of the hotel, a grinning man said to me, "C.D.?" He was a tall, Columbian-looking man with a great dark mustache, and was pointing at his sister as she sat in the backseat of my car.

"Yup, she wouldn't get out the first time I brought her here," I said, pushing the hair back from my face and feeling my stress level at a maximum boiling point.

Isabella got out of the car and I handed her a suitcase that I placed on the sidewalk next to the bellhop. She reached out to grab the handle, then pointed to the large blue plush rug in front of the hotel lobby doors.

The large blue plush rug in front of the doors with a giant yellow H in the middle.

She looked at me. "See? Yellow!!"

Oh my fucking God.

All of that for this? Couldn't she have noticed that the first time?

Then, she dug into her purse and pulled out a flyer from the Hilton. A blue flyer with a yellow H.

"Yellow! Idiota." she said, shaking her head like I was the biggest idiot in the world before slowly walking away from me and heading toward her brother.

"Yes, that's Isabella," Jose repeated as he turned to follow her.

I didn't like Isabella.

I restrained myself as best I could from leaping over her bag and strangling her. She grabbed her bag and waltzed through the turnstile door. No tip, no goodbye. I think she thought that my tip was that I could now distinguish the color yellow.

I wanted to beat her senseless.

Yellow.

Q number 112.

WRONG COLOR, WRONG COLOR, AND WRONG GUY

This might be my favorite story, or at least my favorite topic to talk about.

Communication is a big deal in the workplace; it always has been. Poll most people on what they don't like about their company, it's usually a lack of communication. So, with ridesharing as my full-time business, I try to cut that off at the pass in a hurry. When I receive a notification of a ride, I always text or call my rider to start off on the right foot.

I always identify myself with my name, let them know I'm in a gray Toyota Corolla, and tell them what color shirt I'm wearing. I mean, it's true—I own a gray Toyota Corolla and am usually wearing a shirt with my name on it. I'm doing my part here as best as I can.

On this particular day, it was a red shirt I was wearing as I approached the terminal.

And there was my rider, Martin. Poor Martin.

Little did I know, Martin couldn't tell his colors. After sending my text— *I'm in a gray Toyota Corolla and a red shirt. I'll be there in a few minutes*—he texted back, *OK*.

Now, I usually receive an answer back more detailed answers. This helps us out more than you'd know.

OK is the worst thing I can receive as a text.

You see, pulling up to an airport curbside and having 30-60 people all standing on top of each other, all waiting to be picked up, is like going to buy a fish with your child and having him or her say, "Dad, I want that one."

"What one? Why that one? They're all the same."

People knowing info about you is helpful. Me knowing all the information about you is even more critical. Riders get my information firsthand, anyway; it's all listed on the app, including my name, car style, and even my license plate number. Still, I happen to drive a pretty popular car in a popular color, so it helps, but not really.

So, I feed on your texts, and the more information you can give me about you and your party, the better.

Once, a woman told me, *My husband has a shiny bald head and is wearing a black dress shirt.*

Nice. That's something to work with.

One man had a pipe in his mouth. Even better. Few people have that distinction, especially at an airport.

Another woman said to me, *I have a flowered dress on, red shoes. You can't miss me. I'm carrying a brown knapsack.*

Perfect.

One woman told me she had pink hair and a purple boa. Much more on that later, toward the end of the book.

Gimme some sort of detail to work with when I pull up to the curbside so I can find you. Anything to make you stand out among all of the people there; then I can grab you and haul ass.

People, a lot of people, don't understand that when we come to pick you up that the airport, police are not going to let us park there and scream your name for ten minutes. The police want us in and out and away from that curbside as fast as possible. And most of the time, they're not nice about it. If you're lucky, you can get out of the door, pop your trunk, and yell a name once, maybe twice, before the airport police are like, "Okay, they're not here; move it along."

That's why it can be critical that you call for a ride at the proper time. If you call when you first land, it only takes me about 12 minutes to get to curbside pickup. Chances are, I'll be there before you even get down the escalator and to the baggage claim area turnstiles. Then, I'll be circling the terminal maybe a half a dozen times before you're ready.

Now, you get outside and I can't tell who you are, or maybe you gave me a general description and there are three men wearing jeans with blue sports blazers.

Hell, I've had two women almost get into a fistfight thinking I was their driver, and I wasn't, but I'll tell that story later. Now, ladies, I know that everybody wants me as their rideshare driver, but that's no reason to fight over me.

Martin gave me nothing.

OK, Martin. Be there in a few minutes.

I circled the red terminal three times, looking for him.

I stopped at the curbside, got out, and yelled, "Martin?"

No response at all. Twenty-something people looked at me. Cop yelled at me to move along.

Then my phone rang. Guess who it was?

"Hello, this is C.D?"

"C.D, it's Martin. I guess I got into the wrong car. I got into a red Corolla and the guy has a gray shirt on, just like you texted me."

What's the fucking chance of that happening? I asked myself. *And I didn't quite tell you that. I texted you the right color car and the right color shirt. Hell, you even have a picture of my face and my license plate number on the app.*

I then heard Martin ask his driver—are you ready for this? Talk about a head scratcher—"Is your name C.D?"

"No," the driver replied.

Dude, I'm C.D.

"Is this a Corolla?" he asks.

"No, it's a Camry."

"Ya, I'm thinking I'm in the wrong car," Martin admitted over the phone to me.

Jesus Christ. You think, Martin?

"Okay, so, what ya want to do?" I asked him.

"He's going to pull me back around. I'll have him drop me at the same spot."

"Okie dokie, see you in a bit."

I finally pulled up to Martin a few minutes later and got him in the car. I looked at him through the rearview and raised my eyebrows.

I couldn't help myself. I had to figure out what this dude was thinking.

"So, Martin, when do you figure it dawned on you that you might be in the wrong car?" I asked.

"Geez, well, probably when I called you and the guy in the front seat never answered his phone, but I was talking to you."

OMG.

"That was something. Well, first time for everything, I guess," he said.

Yeah, something.

Q number 107.

ODDS AND ENDS

I don't exactly know where this chapter fits in, but I can assure you it does somewhere in my life, and possibly in others, maybe yours. It's not going to fit like the one card that's turned over facing and the wrong way when you pick up a handful of cards off the floor, but you should understand where I'm going with it.

Being a driver has its price to pay, no matter where you're going or who you're transporting. Gas prices can suck at times, especially depending on the car you drive and the miles during the trips. There are other simple things we go through that normal drivers can relate to. While reading this, raise your hand if any of these things apply to you.

Seriously, you should be able to identify with a lot of these pain-in-the-ass problems that rideshare drivers deal with on a normal basis.

So, no matter if you're reading this on a plane, in a car, or on our leather sofa with what Ms. Ava calls her "blankie"; raise your hand as necessary.

Let's start with being at the pump. I see some crazy stuff at gas stations—long lines, people smoking at the pump while pumping, filling up while the car is running; you name it. I once saw a woman pumping gas and two guys rode by and rolled down the window.

"You can pump me anytime, sweetheart," a guy yelled out.

You should have seen the look on her face. It was priceless.

I find one of my biggest peeves is taking the handle off the holder and selecting the grade of gas. There have been more than a few times that I've had to repeatedly press the grade button. Very annoying.

Sometimes I feel like I'm on candid camera and someone is laughing at me as I push the 87 button over and over, trying to get the action to start.

So, now you've pumped your gas. Time to press yes or no for your receipt. Since you're a rideshare driver, you're running your own business, so it's important to keep receipts for future fun tax time.

You're done and want to leave, yet you get an advertisement for products on the screen at the pump.

Buy 10 wings for $2.49.

I admit this is a nice deal. I enjoy my wings, and some of the best food you can ever get is at hole-in-the-wall gas stations. So, don't get me wrong, but I don't want to see this stuff when I'm ready to leave and go to work. There are enough signs like that in the store and in the windows. Please do not display them at the pump, too; please just spit out my receipt. Branson hates when they're out of paper and can't print—seems to happen to him quite a bit. The poor bastard then has to walk into every gas station and request a receipt. Maybe that explains the sauce all over his lips when he arrives at the lot.

And there's the new pain in the ass debate, if you will engage with me, about our payment technology or, should I say, confusion.

The use of debit or credit drives me absolutely nuts. I pulled into a gas station the other day and it said on a sticker at the pump, "credit outside, debit inside." Why can't we figure out both at the pump so I don't have to go inside? So, I walked inside and the clerk told me to use the machine on the counter.

"Credit or debit?" he asked.

"Well, I can do credit outside, and if I'm in here, then which do you think? Debit," I responded.

"Okay, use that little machine right there," he said.

I put the card in the chip holder. Sounded sensible. I mean, why were chips created for personal security if we aren't going to use them?

That's why we created technology in this world: to make things easier for us.

"Oh, you have to use the swipe," the clerk said.

"But I have a chip."

"Yeah, but we can only use chips for credit," he responded.

WTF, I thought to myself. *So, I can use credit outside, but not debit, and I can use debit inside, but I can't use the chip reader because that's only for credit inside, even though I have a chip?*

Okay, got it. Next day, I'm getting gas and a drink at a different gas station.

So, I swiped for debit.

"You have a chip," the clerk said.

"Yes?" I replied.

"Then why wouldn't you use the chip reader?" He stared at me, preparing for me to punch him in the mouth.

"That's what I fucking said yesterday, but yesterday the chip reader was only for credit," I answered, tingling in minor frustration.

"That's dumb. You have a chip," he said.

I'm still having terrible nightly migraine headaches over chips, debit, credit, and one mouthy clerk who is due an ass-whipping.

Ever dribble your coffee on your shirt while you drive? Burned your chest or lips? Dammit, raise your hand. You've done it.

For select people, have you ever flicked your cigarette out your window and the dead ash blew back in and ended up all over your dashboard? Yikes. Such a pain, and I just cleaned it, too.

I hate red lights. I know their purpose. I get it. I'm even okay with it. But driving down a street when you can see many lights in the distance and you seem to be lucky enough to stop at four out of five red lights, with maybe a quarter of a mile in between all of them? It's a complete pain in the butt. The closer you get, a light turns yellow, and you think to yourself, *let's run it.* A police officer once told my aunt in Boston, yellow doesn't mean speed up and go faster, it means prepare to slow down and stop. He said that just before he asked her for her license and registration and told her to stay put.

Do you wash your hands with soap after you pee, and dry them?

Every time?

Every time!

Want to know how many rideshare drivers don't? How do I know? Sometimes the bathroom at our lot is out of soap for days, and forget about hot water in that portable double-wide port-a-potty.

Please consider this next time you decide to shake someone's hand and thank them for the ride; the hearty handshake, as Justin calls it. It would cost fewer germs to touch tip money and hand it over. If you raise your hand to that one, please go wash after you put your hand down.

Ever been cruising along and someone cuts out in front of you? Even worse, it's a truck that's hauling trash or gravel? And as you slow down, the gravel is dribbling out all over the road, all over your freshly washed car. Sometimes the unthinkable happens and it hits your windshield.

Lots of hands are raised on that one.

When you're driving in the rain, do you put your lights on? You'd be surprised, in all the driving I've done, at how many cars I see not turn their lights on when the darkness arrives and the skies open up and the monsoon rolls in. That's just a little common courtesy. Put your lights on so we can see you. It's not a video game to see how far you can make it during a challenge of blackness and torrential weather.

Another thing that bothers the hell out of me is drivers who don't move over one lane while passing a cop who has pulled over a motorist. You can obviously see the red and blues flashing from a mile away and the police are working with little to no room on the shoulders of the road. Please slide over a lane so they can make sure they go home to their families every night.

Jax always says to me, "I hate when riders talk while I'm trying to listen to the navigation directions."

Despite what people think, we don't know every street and haven't been to every hotel. Close, but no.

Sometimes we're listening closely to the GPS, just like you do when you drive. Then a rider starts talking about their issues and, next thing you know, we're like, "Shit, I was supposed to take that left."

The one thing I can't stand is when people try to get me to avoid looking at the GPS and instead tell me where they live and how to get there. And then they end up telling me to head in the wrong direction. I had a woman in the car the other night; she had lived in the area for a few years and we were heading to her condo.

"Oh, you can go straight here and make a left," she said, as I had my blinker on, ready to take a left a couple ahead of her directions. I started to slow down to follow her command and she pointed from the backseat. "I think," she said. "Well, maybe it's the next left, I think."

Meanwhile, in following her directions, I slowed down a lot and was almost rear-ended because I was trying to make her happy. And all along, I was getting the feeling she didn't know where she was or where she was going.

That has happened so many times, you'd think that I would get it by now: just follow the GPS directions and ignore the rider. Simple. Easy. I mean, it's going to get me there, right?

Does it really matter if I take the first or third left?

Do you really think I care if you have to walk an extra 20 feet to your apartment building?

Can we just get to your apartment complex and not get into a major accident along the way? I'd like to avoid driving down a road and hearing, "No, it's this left. No, this one. No, wait, this one." Just sit back, relax, and let me do what I do. We will get there, I promise.

By the way, what day is it?

I never know. They all run together. That's the one question where someone can get a completely lost look from me every time they ask. That said, Monday nights are great at the lot. Sunday afternoons are, too.

Why?

More science. I do more business during Monday night football or on Sunday afternoons, when the football stadium is full or people are at home or in the bars watching the game. If ridesharing had a vacation policy, those times would be the most popular to take vacation. I also do more business when events are in town—concerts, hockey, you name it. People love to chase events. For some reason, they must believe they're going to get the ride of all rides at the event. Truth is, you sit in a long pair of lines, guarded well by the local police, and wait for your turn. By the time half of the people have exited the event and have gotten in your car, other people exit and get into someone else's car before you get back to the event. Truth is, it's only good for one ride, so I hope that it's a great one. Meanwhile, I stay at the airport and watch the rush of people leave to chase the event and usually get two to three rides in that timeframe. At least one of them usually has surge money attached to it.

You can do well at the job, but I always try to put more thought in it, to make it rise above what I think I can do.

Q number 104.

DOMESTIC DISPUTE

July 8, 8:52 a.m., TPA cell lot.

I finally get a call to start my day and I turn the car on and blast the air. It's warming up quite nicely, probably 90 degrees or so already.

"Have a good ride," Branson says, coming from Q3. He's just trying to capture good karma.

I get "Luck!" from Mathieu, with a thumbs-up as he's eating a cookie and sucking on an OJ.

We all pretty much respect one other and want to see each other succeed in this business. Nobody wants to see someone get a $4 three-minute ride around the corner from the airport to a hotel and then get thrown back into a high Q position that makes them wait for another hour or longer.

"See you in a few minutes," Justin says.

"That's fucking wrong," Mathieu finds time to say in between bites.

I raise my middle finger at Justin as I slowly pull out of my parking spot and cruise away. He grins and responds.

"Have I told you, you look like shit in orange, by the way?" I yell in his direction. All the Denver clothing he wears looks like bile and makes me sick to my stomach.

Cruising up to the terminal, I never know what random odd question I may find the answer to, so, by a show of hands, today we'll find out: does anybody know whether a standard fishing pole will fit in the trunk of a 2016 Toyota Corolla?

For those who answered yes, you're wrong.

I pulled up to pick up a tall young man, Shawn. A black duffle bag was slung over his shoulder and he held a fishing rod. Shawn asked if the fishing rod would fit in the back.

"Nope, but if you roll down a window, I bet we can fit it in the backseat."

We successfully accomplished that.

"So, you're going to Waters St., in Tampa?"

"Yes, sir," Shawn said.

To dispel a myth: drivers don't know a destination until the proper buttons are hit after the rider is in the car and the rider's ID is confirmed. I cannot tell you how many times a rider has looked at me and said, "So, for real, you have no clue where I'm going until I'm in the car?"

No, I do not.

Recently, warnings have been added to inform a driver if it's going to be a 45-minute trip or longer, in case you have a basketball game in an hour or a child you need to pick up from school. But the destination doesn't appear until the correct rider has been confirmed in the car, at which point you confirm the address.

As for Shawn, you could tell he was aggravated. Quite a bit. You could hear it in the tone.

"Okay, we're on our way; here we go," I said.

From time to time, I peered over at Shawn, sitting next to me in the front.

He had a scruffy beard, jet-black hair, and was probably in his mid-twenties. He looked very tired.

"Where did you come in from?" I asked.

"Jacksonville, Florida."

Usually if I get one-word answers, I stop talking, which is hard for me. I like good conversation, especially in the car. It makes the time go by a lot faster.

That's okay, though. Jax always says that he has a few questions to ask and if they all get one-word answers, he turns up the radio. It's a universal sign for "don't bother me."

"So, I hate that bitch. She's crazy!" Shawn suddenly said.

Whoa. Welcome to the party. Okay, now we were getting somewhere.

"She wanted me to move in with her. I refused," he went on.

"Okay, good decision," I said. Not knowing anything about the "bitch," I sided with my rider. He was my guy, after all.

I decided to push the envelope a little bit to find out more. It wasn't my business, but someday it could make a decent chapter for a good book. "What happened, man?"

"For one thing, I never touched her," Shawn said. "I swear I never laid a hand on her."

Okay, that could work one of a few ways, but I wasn't sure.

"I didn't, I swear." He turned to me.

I noticed a stitched gash above his right eye. *Oh boy. Where's Mathieu when I need him?*

"Okay, I get it." I said. "Are you okay?" I noticed fresh blood droplets from the eye.

"Yeah."

He proceeded to tell me about how he and the bitch Laurie—his words, not mine—had a series of arguments while on vacation. Last night had been the final one. He'd followed her to the bathroom after that last one and, as she swung the door to try to get away from him, it had caught him above the eye.

Boom. Blood everywhere. The way he was talking, it had stunned him really good.

Now I was wondering what she looked like. Was he telling the truth?

I was now involved in a domestic dispute situation. Or at least I had heard one side, and I really didn't care to hear the other.

Shawn's phone rang and he answered it.

"Hello, sir," he said. "No, I want nothing to do with her. I never touched her. I dunno how she got the marks on her, but I don't want anything to do with her and I never touched her."

I got that point. He wasn't budging. If he had touched her, he wasn't admitting it.

"That's fine. I have all of my stuff."

All of it? All of your stuff fits into a black duffle bag and a fishing rod?

Shawn hung up.

"Well, I do. I have all my shit," he said, looking honest.

I liked the guy. I wanted to believe him.

Thankfully, at this point, I was pulling up to his place. Another man was on the porch of a small red bungalow in front of us. Shawn opened the back door and grabbed his stuff.

"Thanks for the ride, C.D. I appreciate you listening to my situation."

"No problem. Good luck," I replied. What was I going to say?

Shawn walked slowly up the driveway, toward the man on the porch. He handed him the fishing pole and half hugged him.

"Welcome home, brother," the man on the porch said. The two of them walked inside and the screen door slowly followed them, banging hard against the frame as it shut.

I don't know what happened in that room on vacation and I don't think I want to. I'll never know the truth, that's for sure. Don't want to.

Q number 99 now.

OLDER FOR YOUNGER

I picked Ron up one night at the airport. He was an older man, my best guess is early sixties, and what a character this guy was.

Ron brought arrogance to a whole new level.

He had no luggage, which I thought was kind of weird, having just come out of the airport terminal. He was holding just his cell phone and wallet. He had a swagger to his walk, like a 20-year old, as he approached the car and sat down in the front seat. Some drivers are afraid to have people in the front seat, so they may fill it with stuff, or they might lock the front door. Mathieu always puts a plush pillow in his front seat and tells riders he doesn't have anywhere else to put it, so they have to sit in the back. I don't care whether people sit in the front or back; I figure I'd rather get stabbed from the side instead of by some coward sitting in the backseat. That's just my opinion.

"Hey, how you doing?" Ron said. He had a full smile and looked very pleased with himself.

"I'm good. Where you going?" I asked.

"New Port Richey."

"Okay, let's go. Where did you fly in from?"

"I was in Punta Cana," he smirked. "Great area."

"Looks like you had fun," I said.

"Ya, well, I just divorced my fourth wife. That was my reason for going down there," he said.

"I'm sorry?"

"Don't be. She's a bitch. She pissed me off, so I figured it's time to get rid of her."

I laughed. I can't wait to hear this one. He can't wait to talk and I'm all ears. Some people have that "I can't wait to talk" look, so I ask them a few basic questions and we're usually off to the races.

"The women down there are insane. Just gorgeous women," he said. "And I've been down there a few times and met some great girls. I've found two wives down there. Insanely gorgeous, but not very bright, if you know what I mean. So, this one girl, my now-ex; her kid needs an operation on his appendix, so I ask, 'How much?' And she says, '$40,000.' I say, 'What the fuck? Okay, I'll be down there tomorrow.' So, I'm on a plane and heading down there, and I'm thinking the entire time, how the fuck am I going to pay for this? 'Cause she has no money; not a dime to her name. It's a very poor country down there, but even still, I'm not loaded. Where the fuck am I going to get $40,000? But I can't let the kid die. I can't have that on my shoulders."

"Right," I said. Ron didn't look like he had $40,000, but then again, he didn't look like he had been married to two beautiful women in Punta Cana, either.

"I get down there. I go in. I talk to the doc."

Ron then swung and lightly hit me in the arm to deliver the punchline.

"It's in fuckin' pesos," he said. "I say to him, 'How much is that in American money, 40,000?' Because I don't fucking know. Ya know? And I'm like shitting bricks, because I don't have that type of money. 'That's like $2,000,' the doctor says. I say, 'Jesus. I could have given you my credit card over the phone. I can handle that type of cash. What a dumb slut she is.'"

I started to laugh. This guy was a trip. Degrading to Punta Cana women, but a trip.

"Who needs that?" he said. "There's pussy down there everywhere. I can get rid of her and find another like that."

I waited for him to snap his fingers.

"Look at this one." He pulled out his phone and showed me a picture of a nude girl. Very young. Mid-twenties, I'd say.

"I fucked her last night. I'm telling you, Punta Cana is the way to go if you want chicks. I go down there with my buddy and they're hanging out all over the place, wanting to be wined and dined."

He went on to tell me about all the women he had landed in that area. I thought Ron had good luck in an area that wealthy people would have luck in because it was a poor economy. If only Ron now had the choice skills to maybe find one to stick with.

"I was having sex with this 23-year-old the other night, while getting my divorce papers done with my lawyer. I think I'm going to marry her. Her mom loves me. I bought them a fridge for their house. The appliances suck down there, stupid third-world country. So, I bought them one and they were both so appreciative. Then, as I was leaving, I told her I'd be back in a few weeks. When I told her that, the mother said to me, 'Well, when you come back, I want some.' 'Let's have a threesome,' I said. Unbelievable," he laughed.

Why no luggage?

"I have a place down there. I have what I need down there and have what I need here. Funny enough, TSA didn't understand that. I got flagged four times for suspicious activity. Dumb motherfuckers. Like because I don't have any luggage, I must be smuggling drugs," Ron said.

Ron was obviously enjoying himself in his later stage of life. Some would say, who could blame him?

Raise your hand if you think Ron is just flat-out crazy.

"We rent a car down there, and my ex is driving. Wrong side of the road, 100 mph. So, we get pulled over by the cops. They're like, you're going to jail, and she starts screaming at them in Spanish. I mean really giving it to them. I'm like, 'Baby, this is the fucking cops, and you can't

40

do this.' Next thing I know, she says to me, 'Give me 15,000 pesos.' I'm like, 'What for?' She says 'Just do it.' Cop puts it in his pocket, warns her, and leaves. They just fuckin' want theirs. I'm telling you, what a fucked-up country it is down there," he bellowed.

As we drove down the final streets to his house, we passed an old watering hole that was a good reminder of Ron's nightlife.

"Jesus, I can't believe that no one is there tonight having a drink. Where the fuck is everybody? It's only 11:15 p.m. What's wrong with these guys? That place is always hopping."

As I dropped him off at his house, he told me what a good listener I was. Like I had a choice. He was pretty funny, though.

"Get a sandwich on me," he said as he dug into his wallet and handed me three bucks. I was hoping for a couple thousand pesos.

"What, no 2,000 pesos?" I ask.

He laughed hysterically and shook his head. "What a bunch of dumb fuckers down there."

That three bucks doesn't even by a Big Mac these days, but I'll take it.

Thanks, Ron.

Q number 96.

GROSS

So, in a previous segment, we covered handwashing after shaking the male anatomy, handshaking, and the exchange of money.

It's funny; I always used to go to the mall when I was a child. My father would take me and buy me an ice cream and we'd sit on a bench and do what he called people-watching.

We'd sit for hours and watch people go by, studying their mannerisms and actions. Heck, for simple reasons alone, one of my favorite places is the grocery store. Watching parents yell and beat their kids in the cookie aisle when they throw a fit because they're not going to get their favorite item is funny enough.

Put all of your hands down—I know most of us have done that.

Now, I am, by far, not a racist or judgmental person. My longtime girlfriend Ms. Ava, who I love unconditionally, is a beautiful African-American, as is my good friend, freshly relocated in Virginia, who has probably taught me more about quick-witted humor than anyone I know, and skin color hasn't a damn thing to do with it. He has the punchlines lined up and you can see him scanning in his head at times for which one would be perfect to drop.

My good friends Branson and Mathieu are homosexual men.

I have no problems with mankind or with people's different attributes, yet one thing is simple.

Gross is gross.

I have found people-watching at the airport cell lot to be some of the most top-notch people-watching ever. It totally beats a double scoop of vanilla in a waffle cone while elevator music plays throughout the halls.

I have seen some tremendously gross things.

There's a lady at the lot who continuously walks laps while waiting for rides. She circles the lot in an attempt to exercise, keep in shape, lose weight or whatever, but when she gets a call—bam—she's gone into the car.

For description standards, she's a taller older woman, blonde hair, good tan. Prototypical Floridian. She usually wears jean shorts, a tank top, and flip flops. The blisters she must accumulate on her feet alone make me cringe. I watch her walk at a pretty fast pace during the day. With every lap she makes, she constantly wipes her brow with her palm as she sweats profusely from her workout.

We live in Florida. Ninety-degree days are at a premium. You can only imagine how much this lady sweats each morning. I can't imagine how bad she must smell when her phone pings and she gets into her car to head out for a ride.

Gross.

Jax says to me every other morning, "Can you imagine what she or the inside of her car must smell like on a ride?" He then looks at me, shaking his head as if to say, *how can you not?*

No air freshener could mask that smell. I can give her kudos for attempting to stay in shape. I can even give it to her for maximizing her time and being efficient.

But, gross.

Branson has nicknamed her Stinky. When he gets in the mood, he does 30-second mock air freshener clips.

"When you walk around and smell up your car from a workout, you need this," and he holds up a different aerosol can each time. Where he gets random aerosol deodorant cans from the inside of his car is beyond me.

"You would think on top of that, she'd lose a few pounds off her ass as well," he says. "Just terrible."

He holds his cigarette and keeps on pausing in between thoughts.

"Oh my God, and what horrible flip-flops. I mean, no one wears the ones with the rubber between the big toe and second toe anymore. Just sad, honey." Branson shakes his head.

I have seen enough people who would fit the generic disgusting people email as well. Ever seen that email that goes around from time to time that shows department stores' finest, dirtiest people.

Raise your hand if you have.

If not, look up department store disgusting people images via search engine and have a blast. Just a bunch of disgusting people.

Car washing is a huge thing with rideshare drivers. Many drivers like myself have monthly memberships to car washes and work at cleaning their interiors daily. Take a look the next time you're in someone's car. Some people live in their car.

Not literally. Well, maybe one or two do. I may know one of them.

Enter your vote here for the driver I have already mentioned who could, in fact, live in his car.

Most of us are in our car 12-14 hours a day. Clean is really a good sign. But I have seen some cars where you can edge a "clean me" stick figure into the dust and grime of the back window's exterior. Is that a car you want to be picked up in?

A man or woman with horrible body odor, dirty car inside and out, and stained clothes?

Mathieu can be right about looking poor and getting tipped. But at least he smells clean and showers regularly.

I can tell. You know how you can just tell?

Raise your hand again, class, if you can identify.

Can you tell hat head on a person who looks he hasn't washed his hair or body in days?

Can you tell when a driver has mayo or sandwich special sauce dripped all over his shirt?

Ever seen a person block a nostril and blow out the other all over the ground? What my classmates used to call a gym teacher's snot rag—how many people wash their hands after that? And then, if they don't, they touch everything in their path. I have seen gentlemen with not only consistency in snot-rag shooting but spot-on accuracy as well. Some of them would give Justin and me a run for our money in a game of flick.

One thing I don't like to see is what I saw the other day while I was eating.

I pulled into a chicken and fish place and was sitting in my car having my lunch because the place was mad packed with people. The food is downright good. I don't know what they put in the batter to fry the chicken and fish, but it's downright yummy.

So, I was sitting there, enjoying a chicken sandwich and fries, and I looked over and watched this Class-A beverage truck back up and pull pretty close to the building to make his delivery to the store for the day.

He shut off the truck and wiped his brow, looking like he needed to drink a six-pack of what he'd been driving around all day. For a brief second, I felt bad for the guy. I've driven around different heavy products before, and being hot and thirsty sucks. But I'm not there anymore. So, I accepted watching this man work for his money while I ate my lunch. I mean, it wasn't a hoop game or a decent TV show, but I'd take it.

The man rolled his back door up and disappeared into the trailer for a good few minutes. I was taking one of the last few bites of my sandwich when I saw splashes of liquid coming out of the back of the trailer. I turned the car on and inched forward a little more to see the truck driver with his zipper open, pissing on all of the cans he was about to carry into the store for delivery. At first, I thought, *poor guy. You got to piss, you got to piss.* Then I thought, *ewww, that's pretty nasty that the guy couldn't find time to go to the bathroom in a stall or urinal like everyone else.*

Then it dawned on me. People were going to crack the tops of those cans open and drink from them.

Gross.

This will be the easiest one ever. Raise your hand if you have ever drank from a can soda. You may have been drinking Harvey's piss. Or Billy's or Tom's or Dana's.

Raise them again.

Who is never going to drink from a can again? Or at least wash the top off before touching their lips to a piece of metal that may, in fact, have piss all over it?

Nasty.

Nasty can be the word to describe how cars get after a multitude of rides. Dirt on the floor of the backseat, the sides of the doors, the upholstery, and other parts of the car can get really nasty.

Remember, we live in our cars at times. Eat in them. But that doesn't mean napkins are out of the question or glass cleaner or maybe even carpet cleaner.

I used to have my car cleaned every weekend. Heck, during the summertime, I had a membership to a carwash and used it most days.

I watch most mornings as Mathieu flips his freshly washed jet-black hair out of his eyes while telling his stories. He may play a part to his advantage, but well done, Mathieu. At least you only go so far.

Here's a shout-out to some people who treat their cars so well that they appear to drive in a newer-looking car every time. I've seen some people wipe their cars down with cleaner between each ride— dashboards, doors, backseat.

There have been times where Mathieu and I stare at people as they wipe down their cars and then we look at each other as if to say, "I ain't doing that," and then go back to what we're talking about. Some people are really diligent about using their spare time to keep busy.

Some people write a book.

Others clean their cars.

Q number 91.

COUPLE BUCKS ISN'T BAD

Tipping has always been and will always be a touchy subject when it comes to ridesharing drivers. If a service is being provided, you normally tip. I mean, you would tip a waitress, correct?

A hotel employee delivers your bags up to your hotel room, you tip them, or you tip bellboys, even though I hate them. Bellboys are really good for some things—I just haven't figured out what that is yet. I've had a few run-ins with them at hotels. One tried to take my rider's luggage out of my trunk one night and scratched up the back of the bumper because he couldn't hold the weight of the suitcase. He was a tad undersized, but I think he was a pussy, to be honest.

Taxis, you always tip. Although I did have one man tell me once that his daughter told him never to tip a rideshare driver. When I asked why, he replied, "I don't know."

What, do we not count as service people? I got five bucks out of him when I convinced him it was a disservice not to tip.

I had a rider once tell me that they didn't want to be known as the one person not to tip a taxi, yet their prices are usually 50-75 percent higher than a rideshare.

So, imagine now why a driver might act surprised when he or she receives a "hearty handshake" versus a $2-$5 tip. Some of this can very well be blamed on plastic America, as I call it.

Despite my deep admiration for a cup of coffee, America runs on plastic.

Almost no one carries cash these days and that's an acceptable reason for me at times. I hardly carry cash myself. Yet I have heard and seen stories that would make your head twist around. Or at least they have made mine twist, shake, and, at times, downright vibrate.

The realm of tipping goes like this from a driver's point of view. If you like us and our service, then by all means, I will accept a tip. I'm not going to beg and plead and put a tip jar on my dashboard like I've seen some do.

If you don't tip, don't believe you should, and don't plan on it, that's fine. Don't.

But no driver wants to hear, "Well, I would if I could." My father always told me: if you want to get something done, you figure it out. Get your shit together.

After all, you're getting picked up, having your bags handled and transported, and are being dropped at your door. A couple bucks ain't that bad per bag, you'd think, at least. Even Ron was cool. Didn't understand the value of a sandwich, but hey, three bucks was three bucks, and he carried his own wallet.

So, who stands out the most? Usually late-night riders.

A friend once laughed after hearing me say that if someone really cared about you, they'd be at the airport at 1:00 a.m. to pick your ass up. So tipping a few extra dollars can't hurt to show true appreciation.

With that being said, I have favorites, like Michael.

I drove Michael almost 60 miles to his home and arrived at about 10:00 p.m. While in his driveway, getting his bags out of the trunk, I heard about how he really wished he could tip me, but didn't have cash. If I've heard it once, I've heard it a few times. Then his son and wife came running out to the end of the driveway to see him. If he really wanted to tip me, couldn't he ask his wife for money? I mean, he was home. Go break open little Jimmy's piggy bank and hand me something if you really feel that bad. You can replace it tomorrow. But don't stand there and tell me how bad you feel.

Or there was Lorna.

I brought her and her four bags, which weighed at least 80 lbs a piece, about 40 miles to her house late at night after she flew back in from London. She shared small talk with me about her trip and told me about all the exotic places she had traveled to. I gave her the service she deserved, like all others, rolling her heavy bags from the street up to the garage door, even though I didn't want to. At that point, I kind of recognized it was going to be a short, tip-less goodbye, so I waved good night.

Then she looked at me. "Oh no, dear. Bring the bags to the front door, please."

Biting my lip, I carried them to the front door as she opened up her bag and pulled out two rather thick white envelopes of currency.

"Nope, this has pounds in it. Let me see. I know I have dollars here."

I didn't think she meant that literally, but she continued to search through a couple of white packs, even going through the same envelope three times, as you could tell that the travel bug had gotten her to the very point of exhaustion. After flipping through her hundreds, fifties, and twenties, she turned and handed me $2. Most airlines charge up to $150 per extra checked bag for the flight. Her fare cost her $60; my share was $32. I got a $2 tip. I tip that to the local barista when he's created the best coffee he believes money can purchase.

They're such proud-looking people after they hand you a coffee; they give you that look like you're leaving the shop with one of their children.

Oh well.

Thanks so much, Lorna. I'm so glad you're home safe. How would it feel if your bags hadn't been rolled all the way to your front door? They had wheels. Come to think of it now, that driveway had a slight incline; if I could have only positioned them just right and tugged on them as I left and watched those suckers roll.

She was the only person I ever considered handing a tip back to and telling, "Listen, you obviously need this more than I do." Lorna obviously didn't need the money, but she needed that $2 to call someone who cared about her.

I guess I don't have the luck my buddy Shawn has. After driving a couple to their home late one night, he drove down a long, narrow dirt road to its end. In telling the story, the end was the focal point of a yacht club community neighborhood filled with expensive homes. The man asked Shawn if he had change for a $100. I'd be worried about being bopped over the head and the man running off with my change and his $100 into the dark of the night.

"No, sir," Shawn said.

From the back of the truck, as Shawn was retrieving their bags, the man's girlfriend called, "You're getting some tonight, dear. Just give him the $100."

That's entertainment enough. I would have left there with a smile, knowing that the man was getting some tonight.

The man handed over the $100. Then, on top of that, the woman handed him a $20 out of her purse and told him to buy his kids something special as Shawn had mentioned his two boys during the long trip.

You guessed it. No bags to carry other than outside of his vehicle.

Q number 87.

HEAVE-HO

It's 8:45 a.m., Monday.

"When Jax snaps, we're all going to die," Mathieu always says with a hearty laugh.

See, Jax is the quiet one we're sometimes all afraid of. We've nicknamed him DefCon 5, to go with his military status and all.

When he goes, well, anyone in his path is in danger. In Florida, during the season, Jax can be the hurricane we all watch closely as it turns for our coast and threatens us all. Today it's going to be Sara who encounters the warm stormy waters or turns them into a Cat 5 watch.

We're all sitting around eating donuts, waiting for a call. Mathieu pulls in and stares at us with a mouthful of fries. El Presidente and I are involved in a card game of gin on the back of his truck bumper. El Presidente, better known as Ralph, is the anointed president of our inner circle. Ralph has been the longest rideshare driver of the group. He's usually the first one to arrive at the lot in the morning, and he's always firing up a brown cigar/cigarette, one of those that you kind of can't tell what it is. Sometimes he doesn't even show up to do rides, he just appears to eat a donut, smoke a brown thing, and conduct our "union meetings," which is our universal code word for shooting the shit.

Ralph is a man of few words, but a lot of people seem to listen when he speaks. He studies up on most of the fine-print rules that we all look at but never read. Ralph is the guy who reads them. He's kind of the annoying guy who reads all of the contents and the nutrition facts on the back of something, and then, no matter what the results, he eats the product anyway. He just wants to know every little piece of info that he can digest before trying or talking about something.

Raise your hand if you are that person.

His favorite word is gin. At least around me it is, or maybe I hear that word way too often when I'm around him and just assume it's his favorite.

Jax gets a call and he's about two blocks away from Weston St.

As he pulls into the parking lot, he notices that it's an old hotel building that has been turned into condos, a beautiful building with separate entrances. Jax pulls up in front and has just put the car in park when his phone rings.

"How long before you get here?" the woman asks in a rather nasty tone.

"I'm here now, out front," Jax responds.

"The app says you're not close," the woman says.

"I assure you, I'm out front," Jax repeats.

He gets out of his car and pops the trunk, waiting to see if the woman has luggage.

This woman walks out, a nasty scowl on her face, and says, "What took you so long?" waddling to the rear of the car.

Jax looks at her, puzzled, and says, "Well, I got the call two minutes ago and I was two blocks away; I don't think I was that long. I'm sorry if you thought I wasn't quick enough."

The woman opens Jax's side rear door and proceeds to heave her bag into his backseat, scraping the leather and leaving several marks on the upholstery of the backseat.

Strike one.

As Jax gets into the front seat after shutting the trunk, he notices that the woman is only traveling to Weston St., at an address literally across the street. He asks the woman if the address is correct.

"Yes, can't you read?" she asks.

Strike two.

At this point, the DefCon meter is reaching its limit, but the worst is yet to come.

"And what the hell took you so long to get here is beyond me." She reiterates her thoughts.

Level five has been reached. Hurricane watches are upgraded to warnings in your local Tampa area.

Jax gets out of his car, speechless, opens the back door on the driver's side, and grabs the woman's pink bag. With discus form, he twirls twice and heaves the bag as far as he can, back toward the woman's front door. As it's sliding and scraping across the ground, he can see the already-fragile bag fraying even more. He calmly shuts the door and walks around the back of the car to the passenger's side. Jax opens the rear door.

"Your ride has been canceled. Get the hell out!!"

"Well, I never—and you can't!" the woman says.

"Get out," Jax repeats.

"You will be reported, and I am going to give you a one-star rating!" she barks.

"Okay, and here is your one star, to make sure we're even," Jax says. "Oh, and have a nice day."

As drivers, we do not consider ourselves butlers; we don't deserve to be treated badly or talked to like shit. We're very much human beings. We're offering a service that is paid for, but people should still respect us as we respect them.

This woman was no different than someone berating a fast food employee or any other situation.

Raise your hand if you have ever been berated by a restaurant employee telling you that it's your imagination that your food is cold. Maybe you were treated like shit trying to return something. Or any form of that.

I hate it when someone goes to hold the door for you, whether you're walking in or out, and then they let go of it at an exact moment and you look at them like death. *Asshole* usually is the word you use under your breath.

Maybe if you didn't raise your hand, you're the one who's done the berating.

To make sure it wasn't personal and that nothing was hidden, Jax called his company and explained the entire situation. They got it all on record and apologized to him for the bad experience.

These days, we call any hostile experience with a rider "an opportunity to pull a Jax." He laughs like hell after anyone in the inner circle says it. He called it a day that morning, going home after the incident.

"I couldn't focus," he told us. "The nerve of that woman."

"Gin!" El Presidente says as he throws down his cards on his flatbed tailgate, never even looking at me to acknowledge the end of our game. "You did the correct thing, Jax. Goodbye. Out you go," Ralph says.

"Fuck," I reply, looking down at the hand of cards he dropped to see if the card I needed was in there.

"Damn, he got you again," Justin says. "That man owns your ass at this game."

Q number 84.

CONVICT 2271

Being socially accepted in a group setting is important to most people. It makes you feel good, sometimes more for some than others.

That brings us to Howard. Howard is a great guy at heart. He really is.

I think. I'm not totally sure.

Somewhere deep down inside, his intentions are good. But every group of friends has that one person who shows up and triggers the unanimous comment, "Oh, shit. Look who it is."

That person may approach and you might say to the rest of the group, "How did he find us?"

Then you look at others in the group to blame someone and ask, "Did you invite him? Did you tell him we were here today?"

In this scenario, well, it's a public parking lot. And we do hang out here every day, so it's not actually a mystery where we're going to be and at what time.

But Howard is usually that guy. He approaches and most people say, "Oh, God."

He brings a twist to him. He's off kilter a bit. Well, a lot. Bumming smoke after smoke, asking for loose change to buy something from the vending machines; whatever annoyance it is, Howard is that guy.

Raise your hand if you know that guy or girl in your group. Hell, if you don't raise your hand, take a look in the mirror—you just may be that person.

Although *quirky* and *zany* can be words to describe him, Howard has many delivery jobs. One thing you can definitely say about Howard is that he's a hard worker.

People, food, packages, he's always got several phones going, apps all open, and wears different hats to represent what he's doing. But bottom line, he doesn't know whether he's coming or going, so how should we know? He's always broke or, right to the point, he needs to pay a bill, repeatedly telling us about it.

"I need to pay my electric today. I need $135 today," he says.

We look at him as if to say, "Look, you're a good guy, but we aren't loaning you anything, and frankly, we don't do drama." Heck, shit happens, though.

One time, Mathieu arrived at a gas station and left his debit card on the counter after purchasing gas and smokes. He noticed in the car that he had left it on the counter and went back in to retrieve it. Later, he found out he had been bamboozled for $33,000. Yup.

With most people, if you owe, get out and get your ass moving. If you don't make enough, go do something else to make the money you need. There are no secrets; this is a hustling game. I still feel Howard has good thoughts and a good spirit, so we aren't totally mean to him.

But we're damn close.

He'll make little comments that you know aren't true or aggravate people, and frequently we'll playfully announce we've removed him from our inner circle. Most times, a few days later, he'll show up and announce that he will buy smokes, wash windows, do whatever it takes to be reinstituted.

Playful banter.

Or so Howard thinks.

Yeah, it is ... maybe.

It was a Thursday morning. Beautiful day out. Small number of cars in the lot; it was going to be a good day. Crisp morning.

It was about 6:40 a.m. and Howard pulled up next to me.

Oh, Christ. Here we go.

He got out, disheveled. You could tell something was off.

"Hey."

"What's up?" I said.

"I think I just fucked up," he said.

Okay. I was intrigued.

"What's the deal?" I asked.

"I just left my ATM," he said.

"Okay, and?"

This sounded pretty normal.

"Well, it's a bank that has two ATMs inside the glass door. I'm getting out money, and—"

Okay, stop there. He never has money. My eyebrows rose and I opened my mouth to speak.

"Shut up for a sec and listen. I looked over to the second ATM next to me and there was $800 in the money catcher and a card. So, I grabbed the cash," he said.

WTF? Wait, you did what?

"Wait, you did what?"

"I grabbed the cash. Look."

He rolled out about $800 in $20 bills.

No way, he's never had money. He's never even had two nickels to rub together.

"Dude, where did you get that?"

"I'm telling you, the ATM."

Holy shit. He looked serious.

"Take it back. Why didn't you just walk it into the bank?"

"It wasn't open yet," he says. "And my car payment is due on Saturday."

"You can't keep that."

"I know, but I can't lose my car."

He was going to keep the money, yet he looked like he wanted to cry at the same time.

"I gotta go. I gotta figure out what to do."

The bad part was—well, it was all bad. Where to start?

"You have tattoos all over your arms, man," I said. "Identifiable ones on your arms. There are fucking cameras all over those ATMs. It's just a matter of time before they decide to find you. Wait. What did you do with the ATM card?"

"I left it in the card holder."

Well, at least he wasn't totally stupid.

"I gotta go," he said.

"Take it back," I yelled as Howard got into his car and sped out of the parking lot.

Not 10 minutes later, Mathieu pulled in.

Now, I don't do drama. But this was enough to wet my whistle.

"Hey girl, hey," Mathieu greeted me as he unraveled the plastic covering to a muffin.

"Howard just ... what the fuck," I said.

Mathieu stared at me with a blank look and rolled his eyes. He doesn't like to guess at shit. He'd rather you just blurt something out.

"Howard just showed up here with $800 in his pocket," I said.

"That's impossible; he's never had two nickels to rub together," Mathieu said.

"That's what I thought," I said.

I proceeded to tell Mathieu the rest of the story.

"It's only a matter of time; they will get him." Mathieu shook his head.

"I know. Soon, he'll be wearing an orange jumpsuit with Florida Inmate 2271 on his back," I said.

"For sure. A felony is over $600, I believe."

We didn't see Howard for days, and we were looking. Anybody seen him? Nope.

Almost a week passed before Howard pulled into the lot again.

OMG.

But for a different reason this time.

I was aiding and abetting. I was in just as much trouble. I knew about the crime and never reported it, yet I didn't know what bank he'd taken the cash from or where it was.

Well, I didn't feel that bad, but you never know, right?

He slowly strolled up to the car.

"Hey, guys."

"You're not in the clink yet?" Mathieu asked.

"I bet you'll look good in orange," I said.

"Nope. Okay, so my brother wired me that money. I had to pay my car payment. You guys always have good stories to tell. I wanted one to tell, so I made the whole thing up," Howard confessed.

WTF. I mean, seriously? WTF?

Our stories are real. I couldn't figure out whether I was mad for believing his made-up bullshit story or mad about him lying to us.

This is not a game of one story is a lie and one is real. You choose.

"Well, you're either lying or nutso," Mathieu said. "It's stupid shit like that that makes it so we can't trust you. Not cool. We don't even want to play a part in your garbage."

"So, you're out of the inner circle again," I added, with a more serious tone this time.

"Wait, why? What did I do?" he asked. "Come on, guys, that's not fair. I'll do anything to get back in. You can't kick me out."

He was right; we couldn't kick him out of the lot, but fuck that. I don't need to be involved with anyone who needs to tell a lie about committing a felony to get my attention, whether it's a joke or not.

We don't see much of Howard these days. It's probably a really good thing that we don't.

Oh, and Mathieu and his $33,000?

He stopped one morning at a Quik Mart out in Lakeland to fill up with gas and, I don't know, maybe buy 10 wings for $2.49. No, he told me the story.

He was in there to buy a honeybun and a pack of smokes. He paid with his card, but left the card on the counter during the transaction, a move that would cost him dearly. The store clerk wiped his credit and cash clean by purchasing products to the tune of $33,000.

I remember that day like it was yesterday. In the lot, I loaned Mathieu the $21 I had in my pocket at the time so he could go get gas and run a few rides to make some money. It was hard to get him to even take that. The man has a ton of pride, but for me, it was the least I could do.

It took the bank several days to reverse all the charges and reestablish his credit, but they covered every nickel.

Mathieu had prepared for stupid shit. He had an emergency fund of about $800 stashed away at home, so it would be okay.

Until he got home that night, went to grab his stash so he could get something to eat and repay me … and found out that his husband had blown through the whole $800 on video game purchases.

Continuous nightmare. He was pretty pissed for about a week, but thankfully, it all worked out.

Q number 80.

BUT I WANT TO MAKE THE BOOK, BABE

It was a beautiful Monday afternoon, just after lunch, and I was downtown looking for a ride after just dropping off a business man in the financial district. His $10 tip was rather impressive and had put me in a decent mood. Then I got a call from Rob at a downtown hotel.

Rob and Julie had flown in last night from Dallas, TX.

Rob was a slender guy, into all sports, all the time. He knew his Cowboys, Mavs, and Rangers.

Julie was his wife. A tall, petite blonde, she sported a Michigan hat and also knew her football. They decided to fly in, spend a night out on the town, and were headed out to the beach to stay at her grandparents' place for the week.

After talking with them for a bit, I learned they were newly married, under a year, but totally in love. Their hands couldn't stop touching each other, and you noticed they were in tune with each other's thoughts. Rob was on the phone a few times during the ride and seemingly couldn't wait to get to the apartment because he had a work conference call at 2:00 p.m. Julie was more relaxed, coffee in hand, reading a magazine.

Rob was a joke cracker and liked to laugh. You could tell that he would be the life of the party. Julie wasn't far behind Rob in spunkiness.

"So, I bet you see and hear a ton of shit with people in your car, huh," Rob commented.

"Yeah, I've heard a few stories and seen some stuff. One day, I'm thinking about writing a book," I replied.

"Oh really? Nice."

They proceeded to tell me how they'd met in college. Rob had visited the University of Michigan for a football game when the University of Texas was in town. He'd gone to the concession stand and had bought not one, but two beers "because each beer needs a friend"—his words—and I kind of agreed. In line at the stand, he met Julie and sparks flew. At first they ragged each other about their respective college-wear, but the attraction was more than minor. Spending time in line waiting for a beer can be long and boring, but they made the most of it.

"She couldn't live without me," he said. "Right, babe?" Rob turned and looked at her.

"That's right, babe," she said, and they kissed.

Totally nauseating at first, but they kind of grew on me.

Turned out Rob had the balls to ask for her number and they kept in contact throughout school.

Come to think about it, Rob seemed like a guy who had balls to do anything. Everybody has the college buddy or friend who likes to take his clothes off at a moment's notice or is just that guy you turn to when you need a baseline crazy stunt done.

Raise your hand when you remember that guy.

Despite their college differences, Julie ended up getting a job in Texas, and the rest, as they say, is history. If there were ever two peas in a pod, it was these two.

"So, if you're going to write a book, that's great; you must have seen a lot," he says. "But I want to be different."

Different, I thought to myself. *Okay, this ought to be good.*

"Don't get me wrong, I'm not going to have sex with my beautiful wife in the back of your car."

Thank goodness, I thought.

"Babe, OMG, he doesn't want to hear that," Julie said.

"But I want to make the book, babe. So wait, if I suck her toes, is that good enough?" he lobbied.

My God, please, are we at the beach yet?

"Babe, you would? That's really sweet," Julie said.

Okay, wait. Noooooo toe sucking.

As Julie flipped through her magazine, she came across a *Hot, Not Hot* page.

"Do you think she's prettier than me?" she asked Rob.

Rob never hesitated. "Nope, not at all."

First of all, a fantastic play by Rob, because nothing, and I mean nothing, good can come out of that question. I answer that coming from a much longer marital commitment than these two; I was married 16 years before getting divorced and meeting the beautiful Ms. Ava. You cannot win at answering that question. If you say, "Umm, no babe, you're prettier than the woman in the magazine," then chances are that you're going to get a response like, "Oh, you're just saying that. Come on, really?" If you tell her that the woman in the magazine is prettier than her, you will pretty much get bopped over the head with the magazine and things won't be good.

You can't win.

"Do you think this chick is pretty?" Rob asked me as he stuck the folded magazine up front and pointed to the page.

"Yup, not bad," I replied.

Please, Rob, don't ask me the follow-up question that I think you're going to ask.

Because, let me explain something, Rob: I have zero filter. An ex-boss of mine once said, "C.D. is the guy who says the shit you don't want to hear or don't want to say yourself. The stuff you think, but will shuffle under the proverbial rug."

Passionate, I call it. Hey, I'm from the Northeast; if you don't want to know, don't ask.

Don't ask me to say your wife is hotter than a supermodel in the centerfold of a freakin' magazine. It's not true; we know it. Don't make me lose a potential tip and bring this poor woman in my backseat crashing back down to earth, off the pedestal that her husband so graciously put her up on. It's his job to do so. Well done, Rob.

But don't ask me; it's not my job. My job is to drive you to the beach, dump you off, and head back to get other people, and not judge how hot their wives are. I mean, put it this way: Julie was okay-looking; not a bad-looking girl. I can say it. Remember, I love Ava; we're secure. Julie was okay-looking, but did not belong in a major magazine centerfold piece. Yet, if she did, remember, the episode of the centerfold layout was *Hot, Not Hot.* That means I had one of two answers. Not, *well, she's ehhhh looking.*

So, driving straight ahead, I thought hard for a minute and attempted to cut Rob off at the pass, yet I pushed the envelope a little further.

"That's like the top-five game I used to play with my ex-wife," I told Rob.

"Top-five game?"

"Yup. The top-five celebrities you would choose to have sex with if you met them and the fantasy happened."

So, have you ever played the top-five game? Raise your hand if you have.

Few will raise their hands on this one but I have met some people that have played top five with their spouse. It's easy to have fun with. If you've been married for a while, it also may tell you something about your spouse and their likes and dislikes. Or at least how much they've changed over the years and what type of body or personality they now covet. But, in essence, it's total fantasy. You know, if a spaceship lands in the dark of night in your backyard and one of the five tells you to board the ship and spend a few hours with them and there are no rules and never will anyone find out what the two of you have done.

"So, I can choose any five chicks to get a hall pass with?" he asked.

"Yup, and you have to rank them from one to five," I informed him.

"Oh, this is good," he said. "Let's see. Hmmm."

"What do you mean, hmmm?" Julie says.

"Babe, it's fantasy, you heard him."

"And just who would these women be?" she asked.

Uhh-ohh!!

"Well..." he said.

"You need to think about it? Are there that many? Are there more than five and you have to narrow your choices down?" she continued.

Ohhh goody. Hosin Rd.

"You all enjoy your stay," I said.

"Yeah, fun time," Julie smirked. "Thanks, C.D."

She handed me a $5 bill as a tip. Ironic.

"Get out, lover boy," Julie said to Rob.

"Yup, I have to make my conference call."

Something told me Julie and Rob would have a conference themselves when that call was over. The once impenetrable bond between the two seemed squishy now in several areas.

Uncomfortable was labeled unlucky in my youth's inner circle.

I have mentioned Rob's college buddy status and his brass set of balls.

Crash and burn. College goofballs don't always get glory; sometimes they shrivel up.

   Q number 76.

IT'S MINE. NO, IT'S MINE

Ever seen two people fighting over something and maybe they really don't know what they're fighting over?

Did you raise your hand to that?

At the end of the summer, at the convention center, Downtown holds an huge annual real estate law seminar. It makes the surrounding hotels crazy all day long with people looking for rides, as people come in for four to six days to attend the event.

On this day, I pulled up to a hotel, looking for Mike. I didn't call him to find out what he was wearing or anything because hotels usually don't have the same number of people outside of them as airport terminals do.

I pulled up and there were two cars in front of me, loading up bags in the trunk, people in the backseat. This was going to be rather easy, or so I thought. People do, at times, get, well, aggressive when I'm picking them up. But I never thought I'd see this. Waiting for the car in front of me, I lightly tapped my fingers on the steering wheel. I like to listen to rock and roll and tap to the beat.

Why not?

Most of the time I drive with my right hand forming an 'L' on the steering wheel. If not, my right hand is pinching the wheel with my thumb and forefinger. Being behind the wheel has always been comfortable for me; I've driven everywhere and anywhere. I've only had a minor fender bender—not my fault—since I was in college, and have had few tickets. I've been around the block or two, literally, as people would say.

I'm relaxed with this gig. Life is good. Little stress.

Oh good, they're pulling out.

Time to pull up. I put the car in park, popped out of the seat, and lifted the trunk lever to load any bags Mike might have. Then I started to yell, "Mike!" Immediately, I was greeted by a woman in my face, well, not in the face, she was up to about my mid-chest.

"'Bout time," she said with gusto.

This woman was rather stout, rough, and ready to leave. *In a hurry* was an understatement. Only problem was, I was looking for a Mike.

"Are you with Mike?" I asked.

"I want to put these two bags in the trunk. I'll keep this one with me," she said.

"Are you with Mike?" I asked again.

At this time, another woman had exited the hotel with a rolling suitcase and was headed toward my car, an astonished look on her face. She was a petite woman, makeup done very well, looking very professional. Making eye contact with me, she started to speak.

"This bag, José," she said. "Airport, please? And who is this?" She pointed to the woman in front of her.

Okay, I was pretty confused at this point and, last time I checked, my name was definitely not José. But I was starting to slowly figure out what was up. And somebody, or somebodies, were going to end up disappointed.

Stout was now staring at Petite, and we looked like we were going to have a developing situation.

"Umm, my car, honey. Go away," Stout snapped.

"No. José, tell her to get her bags out of my car," Petite responded.

At this point, I started to smirk, and a man slowly strode up to the car.

"Mike?" I whispered softly in his direction.

He nodded and put his hand up as if to say, "What's going on?"

I started to raise my voice. "These bags need to come out of the trunk now."

Stout stared at me blankly.

"Tell him, José," Petite said.

"My name is not José," I responded. "Stop calling me that."

At this point, Stout turned, looked at Petite, and said, "Get the fuck out of here, honey. You're pissing me off."

"Ma'am," I said. "This is not your car, either."

Both women look at me.

"I'm here to pick up a Mike. Of which neither of you are," I say.

"I can be a Mike," Stout said. "I need to get to the airport, like, yesterday." I didn't doubt her, in some ways.

Sorry about your damn luck, but today isn't your day.

Petite started to turn and walk away.

"God, you're rude," she whispered, and walked over to a bench.

My name is not José, and I'm not here to get you, and I'm rude?

"Mike, can I have your bag, please?" I stretched my hand toward Mike.

"Okay, okay, let's do this. I'll split the ride with you. I'll give you 20 bucks in cash," Stout told Mike.

"Ahhh, no thanks," he said.

$20 to him? This is my car! Where's my kickback offer?

Brutal.

"I'll do this alone," Mike told the woman.

"Some nerve," she said as she grabbed her bag. "I didn't want to travel

Q: Snippets from a Rideshare Driver

in your piece of shit car anyway." She turned to me. "That's right, piece of shit," she repeated as she pointed to my car.

You can't tell what car you're getting into, yet I drive a piece of shit? Funny, that shit piece was good enough to get into 10 minutes ago to bring your sorry ass to the airport, you stupid mother ...

"Get in, Mike," I finally said to my correct passenger.

I started the car, shaking my head, wanting to have more words with that lady. She'd managed to strike a nerve, yet it was very humorous.

I never lose it. It's just a job; it's nothing personal.

Mike turned to me and grinned. "I was going to jump in, but for some reason, it looked like you had everything under control."

I laughed out loud. Few make me do that, but that was funny.

It was worth the show.

Q number 72.

PONDERING THE DRIVE-THRU

Sitting in a burger drive-thru fast lane one Sunday afternoon, I had certain random experiences roll through my head about things I've seen and done in the car.

I'd been brought here by a rider, Shellie. I picked her up from the airport and, after she told me she was hungry and wanted to stop for food, she said she was headed to a family gathering today and wanted to grab a quick bite first. That made sense, as people can be rushed and not have time to eat. Today, she explained to me, was her Uncle Leon's 72nd birthday and the family was having a pool party and cookout in Dunedin, FL. It was a yearly family tradition. We were going to her sister's house to drop her off and then they would head over to Uncle Leon's. Sounded like they were going to have a few drinks, listen to some music, and dance the night away to celebrate Uncle Leon's birth.

How nice.

As we were three cars away from the loudspeaker, inching closer and closer, Shellie extended a $20 bill from the backseat. She seemed hungry and anxious. Maybe she wasn't excited about seeing her family or maybe she was really excited about having some fast food grub.

"I want a 20-piece chicken and four cheeseburgers," she said, exhaling calmly. "Oh, and a diet soda?"

WTF, I thought to myself, *a quick bite? That's not a quick bite. That's a meal for a family of four, or a mega power meal for one.*

And a diet soda? Let's not even mention the fact that she completely forgot the fries. How do you forget the fries?

I hoped she wasn't going to try to eat this in my car. What is it with people who have been sitting down on a plane, sitting in the airport terminal, and sitting and waiting for their baggage, and the first thing they like to do is open up and eat a snack in my car? You have basically had all of this time to sit down and eat and drink whatever you want, make a mess in someone else's area, and you want to decide to eat and drink in my car. I can't even tell you what the slob ratio is for the people who decide to eat during rides. You hear the bag or wrapper rustling in the backseat and the immediate thought is, *I'd be perfectly okay with you eating in my car if I was guaranteed not to have to clean up a mess*, but the slob ratio in my car is at least 90 percent.

At least. And most of those incidents are grown men and women.

I don't particularly care about the reimbursement I get paid for someone making a mess in the seat, although Justin sees it as extra revenue. First of all, you need to take pictures of the incident. Next, you need to clean the mess up, and finally, you usually have to argue with the company you work for about the severity of the spill and how it caused you a major inconvenience. So, just don't eat or drink in my car. Go make your mess somewhere else.

The best thing is when after they make the mess, they look at you and say sorry, like they're completely stunned. It always happens with the short car rides, too.

Can you seriously not wait 7-10 more minutes to eat?

Destroy your living room or kitchen, not my car.

As for Shellie, I was now thinking she was bringing some of this to the party. I couldn't judge; it wouldn't be fair. It could very well be true, and that was an awful lot of food for one person, but I couldn't judge.

Just don't eat any of it in the car, please.

More on Shellie later.

Q number 71.

TITS FOR TIPS

It's always funny to see certain women at the airport doing rideshare.

A select few come dressed for the occasion. One particular woman Jax used to watch was "the SUV girl," as he called her. We never even got her name.

She never showed up a day without six-inch heels and the tightest pants a woman could buy. She would always come to the yard with an open blouse and something covering it, the point being that in summer it was usually 97 degrees; she had enough clothes on to cover her spots, but really had very few clothes on.

"Oh, Tits for Tips?" Justin says now every time we mention her.

We laugh all the time when he says it, but he's right. I'm sure that was her plan.

I guess I was once lucky, you could say, to follow her up to the terminal to watch her techniques. She pulled up in front of two guys, popped the trunk, and got out. Walking in heels so tall that she had trouble balancing her small frame, she stood and held the trunk open as the guys lifted their luggage up into her SUV hatchback. I'm surprised she never broke her ankle.

I watched for a few minutes, wondering. If this was a service, she might drive, but the boys were going to do all the hard work. Somehow, I didn't think they'd mind, given the scenery.

In the car, women frequently talk about their fears of ridesharing. Commonly, they discuss the fear of being in a car alone with a strange man, or the dangers of driving around a stranger.

I usually share a few of my rules with prospective drivers. Hopefully, it makes their decision easier. I always tell people that my first day I drove, I did it on a Sunday morning in a very local area where I knew I could drive around and not get lost. Here comes my science again. I drove on Sunday morning for a few reasons. I chose to drive in the morning, not at night. I didn't want to get introduced to the crazy side of driving when the potential freaks could be out lurking around, causing issues. Sunday morning is also full of church travelers and family members meeting others for brunch or late breakfast. It's a calmer crowd, so I was less likely to have issues on my first day. I also told quite a few people that it was my first day, to break the ice and tension in case I had any app issues or first-time questions; nothing ever goes smoothly the first time. When I told this to the prospective drivers, most women nodded and understood my logic about when to start and what to do. Then I told them, when you get a few days under your belt, head to the airport for more science-related pickups.

It's my view, not a law. Do what you want, but for me, it was easier to break into an unknown that way.

As for the SUV girl, well, Branson got his kicks on her as well. Kind of, but no deodorant commercials; she looked too done-up for those.

"You see, I like her shoes, but honey, those pants are too tight," he giggled. "You can't expect to wear pants like that if you don't want to be called a whore in this cash business, but her shoes are to die for."

"You only wish you looked that good in a pair of leggings, Queenie," Mathieu responded as he chewed on a chocolate bar. "I have to pee," he added, and turned to me. "Want to take a walk?"

"You can't pee by yourself?" I asked. "Because I ain't holding anything."

"Bitch, please."

"Okay, Junior, I'll walk you to the bathroom, but do not talk to anyone in the stalls," I warned.

Somehow that reminded me of my younger son, Alexander, who's 11 years old. His rides are always free and he's my toughest customer, biggest fan, and harshest critic.

I always get a phone call or a text each night I'm driving.

"How many tips did you get today, Dad?" he asks.

It's so funny, but slowly, I think he's actually starting to understand the business side of it.

I can book $200 in fares in a day, but if I receive one $10 tip or $25 or $30 in tips for the day, I'm a hero.

Then I hear a young voice on the other end of the phone saying, "Well, nice score, Dad."

Alexander was born in Detroit, MI. My oldest son was born in Salem, MA. We've bounced around a bit as a family, living in different states. I love the Florida weather, but Boston will always be home.

Many riders have given me shit for living in other areas and now settling in Florida; mostly sports fans. Some have praised me for making the choice to move to the Sunshine State and, of course, some have asked what took me so long to get away from the cold, snowy weather.

One sports fan I recently had in the car was rather hostile.

"You know, all of the Northeast sports fans can just, well, excuse me, but they can just all fuck off," Kevin said to me in the car one day. We were headed to St. Petersburg to take him home and struck up a conversation about the hometown baseball team and the lack of attendance they drew.

"They come down here and enjoy our sunshine and the weather, but they don't back our sports programs. That's ridiculous. They wear the clothes of those teams, they talk in those funny accents, and for what? If you don't like your weather, too bad; stay up there and back your own frigging team. I'm sorry, but that's the way I feel."

This all happened in the first few minutes of the car ride. Then, Kevin settled into his seat and got comfortable.

"So." He peered over his bottle-cap glasses at me. "Where are you from?"

Really? I couldn't wait to tell him. Your stadiums are usually only filled to capacity when my team comes to town. If it wasn't for the number of transplants down here, attendance would be non-existent.

Most people listen to me talk for a minute before asking how long I've been here. A good chunk of riders are transplants coming down for business. Quite often, I get Northeasterners in the car and the weather is the first thing they comment on because it's usually a violent change from where they came from.

Kevin just sounded like he'd had enough and was going to lash out at the first person he ran into. He'd probably been picked on his entire life and, lucky for me, he'd had an epiphany just before he got into my car. The car with the Red Sox sticker on the back of the trunk, which he apparently didn't see.

Alexander, on the other hand, always earns his share of the pie. Many times, he comes over to help me on a Sunday morning, and we vacuum the car out and wash the interior and windows. In return, I buy him a cold fruity slush or soft drink of his choice. Sometimes he puts the dollars in his pocket and waits it out until he sees something he really wants, but he's 11. It never lasts very long because he always spends it quickly, but he always knows how to work a dollar out of me.

It amazes me the choices that some of my riders make in regard to their children, such as not having a car seat when I'm transporting them. I've had many parents try to get me to do that. I don't carry a car seat because it takes up potential luggage room and I usually only get one or two little children a week, so there really is no need. I would never have tried to transport my children in a car without a car seat when they were younger. Ever. Even just down the street to a store. I don't know anyone who would consider it safe to put young kids in the car with no car seat, and I'm talking infants to three years old.

But the other day, I picked up a woman named Cecilia at the blue terminal, and as I curled around the corner to pick her up, I knew what I was in for as I saw a young woman at the terminal, standing alone, with an infant in a swaddle attached to her chest. I didn't even bother to put the car in park or hop out to look at her luggage. I just pulled up next to her and cracked the window slightly.

"I'm Cecilia," she said. "You C.D.?"

"Yes," I answered. "But I can't take him unless you have a car seat for him. Do you?"

She just stared back at me, a blank look on her face.

"Do you transport him at home without a car seat?" I asked.

"No."

"Then why do you think I would do it in my car?"

Even if I didn't care about the baby and whether we got into an accident and the little guy was jolted out of his mother's hands, tossed around in my car, or thrown through a windshield, there was the factor of a police ticket, which is not covered or reimbursed by my rideshare company and the guilt over making a completely stupid decision. Does anybody get where I'm going with this?

Maybe a show of right hands? If you're not raising your hand on this one, well, let's just say this is a hard one to not raise your hand on.

I don't understand where people get over trying to suggest it. I don't understand where people get over trying to get me to assume the responsibility. I flat out don't get any of it at all.

You would really be surprised at how many times I've been asked to attempt it. I'm sure that someone will pick up Cecilia and her baby, let them sit in the backseat, and watch her play, entertain, or comfort her baby in the car without him strapped down in a government-approved, fire station-checked, properly weight-structured seat. The driver will try to make it to their destination without getting into an accident or risking a ticket.

I left Cecilia standing at the blue side terminal that morning, though. I had no problem doing it, and it had nothing to do with jokes or laughter.

Q number 69.

COURTESY OF YOUR FOOD PROGRAM

So, along with people ridesharing, there are other demos we've been working on with the company. One of them is the food delivery program.

Just after starting with the company, I got a message on my phone telling me how cool the food program was and how it was a great way to make extra money. All you needed to do to participate in the food program was to tell them yes by clicking a box on your phone. You'd then be eligible to receive calls for delivering food to people.

Never once when I was younger did I ever want to be a pizza delivery driver. Now, at 47, I fully understand why. Food can be such a complicated thing to bring to people.

First off is the temperature. If it arrives and it's cold, you have an irate person on your hands. People, for the most part, always think they can do things better than you can, especially if they're paying for it. The downside of this program is that the customer isn't actually with you. They don't see the red lights that cause delays or the slow clerk putting the order together while you're standing there waiting for it. They can see on the phone that you may be waiting, but unlike a rideshare, they don't experience firsthand that there's a delay. Some food doesn't taste as good cold as it would have hot. The sogginess of once-hot food can be an issue for the customer.

I was in St. Pete on a Tuesday afternoon in July and got a call to pick up a basic fast food meal—hamburger, fries, drink, and a chocolate sundae.

Yes, a chocolate sundae in warm, steamy, muggy Florida.

This woman lived eight miles away from the location, so you can imagine what that chocolate sundae looked like when I showed up 15 minutes later.

It looked more like a bowl of black and white soup.

I arrived at the door after traveling through traffic to get to this woman's house. It was a warm day. I mean *warm*.

It took several knocks at the door to get someone to answer my call. The woman who answered had a screaming baby on her hip. Not a good start.

First thing she commented on was my tardiness.

"Took you long enough to get here," she said, as she tried to grab the bag of food. I noticed a car in the driveway and immediately thought to myself, *if that thing works, you could have gone to retrieve your own food.*

"And what is the deal with my sundae, man?" she bellowed.

"Got it here as fast as I could," I said. "But it's Florida, and it's hot."

"Don't you have AC?" she asked.

"Very good AC," I replied.

"Obviously not that good," she remarked.

I turned to walk away and thought to myself, *screaming baby, very hot day … people have a right to be miserable, I guess.*

That wasn't the only bad experience I had with the food program, but trust me, I didn't participate in it for very long. I had other instances that were very similar to that one.

No tipping, lots of grief, and bad attitudes lead the list. Transporting people is by far and away the better of the two jobs.

There were a few not totally horrible scenarios in my very short food delivery career. I once drove a hamburger one block after I picked it up in the much-commercialized area of Ybor City in Tampa. When I arrived and gave the meal to the woman, she was very happy. She was standing in the front lobby as I arrived at the door.

"It's so hot; I'm not going out there," she said to me, although she did hand me $5 extra.

I couldn't help but laugh at her spoiled-rotten ass. If you don't want to be walking in a hot climate to get lunch, move to another climate. Get a car, do something.

Another annoying part of the food delivery program was the occasional times where, upon arriving at the location, people weren't home to accept delivery or refused to answer the door.

Protocol in the work chain was to notify customer service and inform them the person was a no-show. Once you did that; customer service would try to notify the customer. I don't know why, because I was standing in front of the address with a phone number and I couldn't find them.

What made them think they'd be able to? Unless they had some sort of locator beacon on the person.

After the grace period of customer service trying to find the people, sometimes you would get a message to dispose of the food. So now you had to find a trash barrel or drive to a location where you could throw away something you picked, tried to deliver, and now were not going to get paid for.

Some of the drivers I know will take matters into their own hands.

"Did you hit that?" Justin asked as we played another game of Flick the Butt, with the green stick sticking straight up out of the concrete pole as the target. It looks more like a skinny foul pole in right field.

"I think so, but I'm not sure. Do over?" I yelled.

"Yup, okay. That's fair," Justin said.

"It looked right on. Damn wind," I said. I hit it, but I wasn't in the mood to really argue about it today.

"Here comes Mathieu," Justin commented.

"Hey girl, hey," I said as Mathieu's car pulled up alongside of me. I noticed he had a mouthful of something, and you know how much we like to eat.

"Hey girl, hey," he said. "So, another food delivery. Love it. They didn't show up. Call customer service and wham, I got fries and a sandwich. Boom, free breakfast."

"What? You ate the friggin' fries?" I asked. "Can you do that?"

Justin shrugged his shoulders. "I mean, I guess; why not? They told you to get rid of it." Justin always has a diplomatic way of looking at things.

He kind of had a point.

"What was the order?" I asked.

"Burger, fries." Mathieu held up his right hand. "Oh, cold Sprite." He sipped out of the straw. "Courtesy of your food program. I love this shit. I'll do them. People hate them. I'm getting at least one free meal a day."

"I mean, why not?" Justin replied. "Jury favors the defendant."

"I guess I can see it," I said. "They did say dispose of it, even if it's not clearly disposed of in your belly."

"Honey, your fries are getting tasted by the quality assurance program, whether they get delivered or not," Mathieu said. He admitted that if he could taste something out of your bag and have it not be noticeable, he was going to do it.

"What?!" I said.

"That, yeah, umm, that's wrong," Justin said. "I think—pretty sure—that's wrong." Then he started to laugh.

"I can't believe I hang out with you people," I said.

"Oh, calm down," Mathieu says. "You'll be okay, sweetie. It's just a few fries, and in this case, it wasn't even a delivery. They refused it."

"My turn," Justin said, as he finished the last drag of his cigarette. The wind, of course, had calmed down. Figured.

"Who's ringing?" I asked. "That's a phone, hear it?"

"It's me," Mathieu said. "It's Jax. Hey girl, hey."

You could hear Jax speaking through the phone because Mathieu had switched him to his speakers via Bluetooth.

"Hey, so I just got a food delivery and no one's home," Jax said.

"Oh, God," Mathieu cheered. "Eat it."

"They just told me to dispose of it properly. Is that what you all have been doing?" Jax asked.

"Not all of us," I said.

"Some of us," Justin said. "But I guess if you're hungry and you're told to dispose of it, then WTF?"

"Eat it. Eat it. Eat it," Mathieu chanted, fries in his mouth, reaching for his drink.

"I got to admit, it doesn't look too bad, it smells great, and I'm hungry," Jax laughed. "It hasn't been in anyone else's hands except mine. I know it's okay."

Raise your hand if you would eat it.

Don't worry, no one's looking anyway.

Q number 66.

OLD SPORTS

I always enjoy talking sports with riders. My girlfriend is jealous at times when I watch and talk about sports.

"I wish I loved something as much as you love watching the games," Ms. Ava says from time to time. She should love me just as much. I know I love her more than sports because she can ask me if I want to do something during a game, or knowing that a game is on today, and I'll shut the game off or not watch one at all so I can hang out with her. But she's right that at one time, it was always:

1. Breathing.

2. Baseball.

3. Football.

4. Women.

Many riders come in from different cities, great sports towns, and we talk about their managers, their ownership, and their line-ups, but I have definitely had a few in the car who act like general managers of their teams but clearly don't have common knowledge to make quality decisions.

Like Oscar from Cleveland.

Oscar was a great guy and a hell of a sports fan to talk to. He knew the history of the games, the different teams, and was very knowledgeable on the home front as well as the national scene, and then he completely dropped the ball during the conversation.

The baseball team in Cleveland had been on an incredible winning streak in the fall of 2017. They'd won many games in a row and had lost only once in a month. Not really a big deal, as Oscar was telling me in the car on his trip out to Clearwater to spend the weekend at the beach and go deep-sea fishing.

"I tells ya, C.D.," he said, and by the way, I didn't write that wrong. I'm not going to write this wrong, either. "Any team that wins 25 out of 24 games is remarkable."

Did you just say that the baseball team won 25 out of 24 games? It's a mistake; it has to be.

So, I repeated, "25 out of 24, huh?"

"Yeah, you heard me," Oscar says. "Hell of a streak."

Wow, he said it and he meant it. How the hell do you win 25 out of 24? You can't. It's mathematically impossible. Am I missing something?

Raise your hand if you're with me on this one.

To make things worse, he was an accountant. Can you say audit?

I don't know, maybe it was a Cleveland thing. I mean, they have been really popular these past few years in baseball and basketball.

So, as alarmed as I was with Oscar, I couldn't help but also smirk at Burt. Burt was, like Oscar, a class-A Cleveland fan.

He knew his shit. Just ask him, he'd tell you all about it.

He loved his football, which in Cleveland is an odd mixture, but he loved it, anyway.

Scary. He didn't know anything other than football. Anything.

So, I said to him, "Hey, the Cavs, man. Won a title, finally got one. It's great your city is exploding. Good for all of you."

He looked at me and got all serious and said, "Oh, the Cavs? I don't watch baseball."

Oh my dear God.

I had an elderly couple in the car from North Carolina a few weeks back. The woman in the back of the car asked me where I was from.

"Boston," I said.

The woman looked at me and said, "Oh, how are the Packers doing this year?"

Her husband, about 80, looked at her and said, "You dumb bitch, where did you get the Packers from? That's a team in Green Bay."

I rarely laugh, but this time I couldn't help it. And the two of them were still going at it and not paying any attention to me.

"Why did I think that they were from Boston?"

"He is. He just told you that," the man said.

"The Packers, you asswipe," she scowled back.

"Because you don't know football from shit," he said.

Her look could have burned through lead.

That was funny.

Elderly couples are cute and funny. Just as long as they don't smell or get sick in my car.

I drove another elderly couple to the airport from their Clearwater high rise condo one early Friday morning. They were trying to make the 6:00 a.m. flight.

It was 4:23 a.m. and we were headed over the bridge into Tampa. It was windy and raining like all hell when the husband got a call.

"Hey Gary," the man said. "Good to hear from you, too. No, I can't play golf this weekend, we're headed out to England today for two weeks. Okay, well, thanks for checking up on us, Gary. Everything is great. Call you when we get back."

The man's wife was sitting in the backseat, rubbing gloss on her lips, in fairly close proximity to the phone call.

"Umm, so who the hell is Mary, and why is she calling you at 4:30 a.m.?"

"It's Gary, your son?" the man said. "Jesus Christ. Really, Agnes?"

"Oh, Gary. How is he?" she asked. "Did you tell him I said hi?"

The man looked over at me, slightly turning his head, and stared into my eyes as if to say, "Do you know how long I have been putting up with this?"

We never had to share a word on that topic. His eyes said it all.

Later on another ride, a woman from Kansas City basically held a State of the Union address on her sports teams. Funny thing was, her husband never flinched or added anything, come to think of it.

Anne went on and on about the Chiefs switch at quarterback, filling the holes on their offensive line, and the running back they had just drafted. She went on to talk about the baseball team and even broke down a few of the pitching prospects in AAA that the Royals are set to bring up in 2019.

I steered the wheel with my mouth open for half the ride. It was pretty cool to see a fan in a small market break down her love for the games and know her shit.

I was listening to local sports radio at the time of the car ride.

"Rays and Royals at the Trop tonight, starting at 6:05 p.m., and the local squad, well, they need to get the bats going tonight as they face a really tough pitcher," the radio host said.

"They don't have a chance tonight," Anne said. "Kansas City has the lowest WHIP of anyone in the month of June." WHIP is baseball terminology for total number of baserunners allow per inning.

I turned and looked at Anne's husband. He nodded, as if to say, "That's my wife." I think he also knew the information but didn't have to say it because she already had.

Nice job, Anne. Way to come into the car swinging and have your shit together.

Q number 61.

GIRLS, TREES, AND BALLOONS

I picked up a few men returning to London, England, after being downtown at a seminar.

It was a Thursday afternoon. Great weather outside, and the scenery fit just right.

They were very proper speaking as they held a light conversation about work, yet the one sitting up front with me never really said much. I love their accent. I mean, people often tell me that they love my accent—I still have a bit of it. It's not as strong as it once was when I lived at home, but these boys still lived across the pond and their accents were still very strong. One man just stared out the window, his head snapping back quite a few times during the car ride.

No drugs are allowed in the car. Joking, but seriously, no drugs.

He wasn't on drugs, and I didn't really understand his motive until we got out at the end and he handed me a five-dollar bill.

He looked at me and smiled. "You know, emmm, you all have unfair odds in this city."

"We do?" I said, not totally understanding yet.

"Why yes. The woman are exquisite in this town and so many of them at that. The odds for you men are totally unfair. We don't have women like this in Europe on the streets."

First off, were the odds totally fair, or totally unfair? They're not unfair if there's an abundance of beautiful-looking woman in the greater Tampa area and we men have such a large choice to pick from. That's a great problem to have, not totally unfair.

But, not my problem; don't live in England then. I'd say the odds are great, not unfair, and don't move here because that will decrease other men's chances in Tampa. But I'll invite him, anyway.

"I don't know what to say, ol' chap." I attempted to make fun of him over his head. "If you don't want to live in England, emmm, move to Tampa. But I hope you enjoyed your stay."

I'm out of here. I'm not interested in listening to your ass complain about the quality of women in your country, but thanks for the compliment of how good we have it. I think many men in the Tampa area would agree with you.

I've got money to make and you can live anywhere you want. No tea and crumpets here, but plenty of bangers and smash.

I remember one day I came up around the bend for a pickup at the airport. Early Sunday morning, I was trying to get a few rides done before football started, make a few extra bucks to get real wings at a wing house, not 10 for $2.49.

I was headed to blue terminal to get someone and sent my usual message saying what car I was driving and what color shirt I had on. I waited a few minutes and had moved closer to the terminal when I received a text.

The girl, Donna, sent me back a picture of balloons and the word "congrats."

WTF?

Congrats to me that I'm driving a gray car and have a blue shirt on? Reminded me of those times in high school and college when someone would say something and you'd respond just to be a dick.

"I just bought the newest fighter game on my gaming system," someone said.

You responded, "Proud of you." Just to be a dick.

Raise your hand if you ever did that. Don't be afraid. If people are looking at you, they don't understand it was because you were being a dick many moons ago during high school or college; they just see you raising your hand.

Anyway, so yeah, this woman sent me a picture of balloons.

Congrats that you're in a car and blue shirt, coming to pick my ass up because I don't have a ride. Nobody loves me enough to give me a ride; I have to pay for one.

It took me all of 2.6 seconds to cancel that ride. Shocking abuse of my power and authority.

But I'm a grown man now, doing this for grown-up reasons like paying my bills, providing for my children, and writing a book about funny stories and some of the great people I've met. She was not one of them, but great news for me—I never met her.

She made the book though, as Rob would say.

I sometimes think of that one and wonder, if I had proceeded with the ride, whether it would have been funny and just a bad attempt at humor or if it would have been hell and a handbasket.

Hell and a handbasket? I don't know, my grandmother always used to say that.

Heck of a way to reassure a total stranger who is picking you up and driving you somewhere that all of your marbles are secure.

Just after I started this gig, one rider actually said to me, "If you had someone who loved you or cared for you that lived here, you wouldn't be having a stranger give you a ride to where you needed to go."

That probably fits with 60-70 percent of the people I drive.

You'd be surprised how many people are home when I get people ... home.

That wasn't like Josh, though. He was going home and he was excited as hell.

I was driving in downtown in Tampa one day, getting ready to pull up on a hotel, and I texted Josh.

I'll be there in a few minutes. What are you wearing?

He responded, *a black hat and blue jeans, standing on the curbside of the hotel.*

As I pulled up outside the hotel, I saw a man in his thirties, black hat and blue jeans, looking straight up at the sky. Just looking straight up for about five solid minutes. Enough to the point where I stopped the car, put it in park, and also looked out the window, straight up.

I didn't see anything. *Maybe he's thinking? Listening to music? I don't know.*

So, I beeped the horn and he made his way across the street and opened the passenger door and said hello.

"What were you staring at?" I asked.

He smiled. "I was looking at the palm trees," he said. "I wanted to make sure the image was in my head for a while to explain it to my girlfriend."

"Where are you from?" I asked.

"Vancouver, BC. Don't see any palm trees up there," he said. "So, of course, my boss asked me if I wanted to go to a convention in Tampa, FL, and I said hell yes," he laughed.

"Wow, very cool," I said. "What do you do?"

"I design and build bars. We sit down with the owners and put the image of the bar on paper, then they find the real estate and we build out what they envision. My girlfriend is up in Calgary with her friends on a snowboard and hiking trip. This weekend will be the first time we've seen each other in a month."

"I hope you get your first few drinks for free when you complete those bars?" I laughed.

"I'm owed a few drinks all around the country," he responded. "But I had to bring her my vision of a palm tree. Neither of us has ever seen a palm tree before. It's pretty exciting."

Whatever. It's just a tree.

Q number 59.

DRIVING THE STARS

I've picked up a few sports stars and their girlfriends.

I had a hockey goalie, a nice young man who had just been traded to the local hockey team in Tampa and was checking out schools for his kids because he was trying to get established in the area. I picked him up right outside in front of the arena that day. He was just an average-looking guy. It was pretty neat to meet him and discuss kids, as we both had little ones.

We never once talked hockey, yet you could just tell that he was a hockey player. I'm not one to infringe on people's professions and ask for an autograph or a photo op. He asked about other local sports players and where they lived in the Tampa area. It sounded like he was house shopping. Funnily enough, he had come from a cold weather climate team and now, experiencing Tampa, he sounded like a happy dude.

I also picked up a political analyst from a major cable news station. What a great story, and maybe one of the best conversations I've ever had with someone in the car. We really talked nothing about politics, and the ride was only about 20-25 minutes.

It was one of the rare times I allowed myself to receive a call after dropping off a person from the airport. I don't usually do that, but the airport was slow, so I figured, why not?

I was driving down in the Davis Island area in south Tampa, where some of the stars live, and I was looking for address 95. I saw the mailboxes and started counting. It's a little trick they taught us way back when I was a delivery driver.

89

91

93

Found it, 95. Nice—beautiful large house on the water.

I pulled past it and reversed up into the driveway. I parked in front of a huge, beautiful staircase and tapped on the steering wheel, listening to music until my phone rang.

"Hello," I said.

"When you go around the corner, I'm the white house, three houses down," this woman said. "Oh, you're here?"

At that moment, she must have looked up and seen my car.

Of course I'm here. I'm a five-star driver. A professional driver for 25 plus years.

I drive all kinds of products and get them to any address in the country.

I can find a big-ass house with a number 95 on the mailbox.

By the way, big-ass mailbox.

She opened the door.

"I was walking down the stairs, telling you on the phone how to get here, and I looked up and you were in the driveway."

"Yup," I said.

"How did you find this place? Most people can't," she said.

"Well, the mailbox has your number on it and the roads at the beginning have signs on them, so ... yeah." I laughed.

"Cute," she said. "I've had five rideshare drivers out to this house and no one could find it."

Maybe they were stupid. I started to pull out of the driveway.

"Wait, you're a five-star driver," she says. "I've never ridden in a car with a five-star driver."

"Yup, thank you," I said.

After getting off her street, we talked a bit about Boston, where she'd attended law school. After she told me she'd attended Harvard Law—that's where you want to go for law school!—we discussed our other favorite major cities. We talked about what pulled us to Florida and all along, I kept staring at this woman through the rearview mirror.

No, Ms. Ava was not in jeopardy. I knew this woman from somewhere. I just couldn't tell you where.

She told me about the book she was writing and I told her about my desire to write the history that you are reading now. I ended up dropping her off at a wine-tasting bistro in south Tampa.

"Good luck with your book, C.D." she said. She was the nicest, most pleasant conversationalist I had been with in a long time. As she got out, she thanked me, I wished her well on her book, and she walked in.

It bothered me so badly that I couldn't place her that, when she left, I searched for her first name and channel; she had given me that info.

Realizing now, I snapped my head back and looked again in the rearview mirror. She was one of my favorite political analysts during all of the presidential coverage. She was in my living room many times during the six months of coverage. I just couldn't relate to her face being in my car, so I drew a complete blank.

Good ride. Still, to this day, she's on my screen as my favorite ride and conversation.

And no, Justin, no tip.

Justin is always my tip mate. We sometimes judge good rides by the tip or mention the ride by describing the tip. Justin is my best friend at the lot. I'm close to a lot of the guys, but he is the man. Head cocked to the side and slowly dragging his cigarette, he and I have had great conversations and some even better laughs.

He's just good people.

We will frequently text each other on the road and rub the size of fares or tips we received in each other's faces. He received a zero tip from a professional wrestler once. She was the recognized champion at the time and wouldn't even give him a photo op.

Another one of my favorite conversations was a ride I gave a professional boxing referee. He was in downtown St. Petersburg at a pro boxing referee rules conference. When I picked him up, he was headed back to the airport to go to home to Minnesota. He explained some of the countries he had traveled to and how the promoters for the fight pick a referee. He also explained the travel scenario and the ins and outs of the many details, getting yourself to the arena, checking with the fighters before the fight, the very high levels of championship fights he had been in charge of, etc. We talked about the delicate control he has in the ring of trying to understand when a fighter gets in trouble and when to stop a fight. The amount of responsibility that puts on someone's shoulders is tremendous. In his off-time, he designed borders and frames for personal moments, such as newspaper articles that people have been in, and he turned them into keepsakes. He showed me a few items of his work that he had on his phone. It was so different to see the scales of the work of one person, the physical brutality of boxing, and the calmness of his quiet studio back in Minnesota, bordering some beautiful moments.

Great work, Leonard. He even shouted to me, "You're out!" when he left the car as he prepared to walk into the blue terminal toward his airline. When I put the car in park, I asked him to give me his knockout call.

We're next in line for Shellie, by the way.

Q number 56.

KISSING THE DERBY

Interacting with customers is obviously one of the major things you can do while driving. I remember a couple of days where my interaction was deliberate yet innocent and because of those two days, I now have a couple of enemies.

First up was the couple, Kelly and Ed. They were out on Clearwater Beach on a first date, and I happened to be there on a Saturday at noon, so I picked them up in front of a restaurant.

They got into the car and were really lovey-dovey, and you could tell. I think Ed was a little more into Kelly than Kelly was into Ed, but I wasn't all that interested, so I didn't put much thought into it. It wasn't until I picked them up and started to drive that I understood that I could get some pure, clean enjoyment out of this ride.

So, I began.

"How was lunch?" I asked.

"Oh, it was great. I really liked it," Kelly said. "This is our first date."

"Oh yeah? No way, that's cool. Congrats," I said.

Ed, all along, was licking his lips. Thankfully, not at me, but at Kelly. I don't think Ed had gotten a first date kiss yet and he was ready spaghetti. And I figured it was my duty to fuck with him the whole 7.9 miles to their destination. Someone had to do it; might as well be me.

He was on the move and ready to get her. He grabbed the back of her head and slid in for a pucker.

"What did you have?" I asked.

"Oh, we had blackened fish and sauce. It was great," Kelly said as she pulled away from Ed to answer my question.

Ed looked majorly irritated but seemed to chalk it up as mistiming. He got ready to slide in again for the kill.

Little did he know I was devoted to screwing up this car ride for him just for shits and giggles.

As Ed got really close to Kelly again, I chirped, "Was it expensive, Kelly?"

Pulling away from Ed, she said, with both hands to his chest, "Oh no, I thought it was priced good."

I didn't give a fuck—this was going how I wanted it to—and the looks from Ed in the backseat were precious.

He moved in for another kiss. Well, for the first one he still had yet to receive.

When he was inches away from Kelly, I had to ask, "Did you need a reservation?"

"No!" Ed said, sounding frustrated. "It's Saturday and the place was dead, okay?"

Man, he sounded snippy. Why, I didn't know.

Not my fault you haven't kissed her yet. Or is it?

Guess I had to continue then. He was moving in again.

Bogey at two o'clock. Fireflies everywhere, time to attack again.

"I'm not a big fish person. I mean, I like it, but it's okay," I said.

"Who cares," I heard Ed mutter as it now looked like I'd won and Ed was going to have to wait until the car ride was over.

Kelly hit Ed lightly across the chest with her palm. "It's my fav, and they did it good."

Well, we arrived, and that was pretty fun, about as much fun on the short ride as I thought I could have.

"You all have fun. It's beautiful out today," I said to them.

"Uh huh." Ed stared out the window. Thankfully, though, he tipped me $7.

Do you really think that Kelly would have answered me every time if she really wanted to kiss Ed?

Raise your hand if you do. Not too many hands raised, I see.

Now, let's go to the Derby.

Picture yourself blowing the trumpet, as most famous horse races are known for that sound at the beginning of the day or race.

The horse race of the century, the Kentucky Derby, is usually known for parties, gatherings, dresses, and suits, but more importantly, hats. On this particular day, I was picking up Kenny and Kathy, who were going to a horse racing facility in Tampa to watch the derby and attend a party.

Kathy came out in a blue dress, like a gown. Very sophisticated, elegant, almost looking like she was going to attend a wedding. As she got in the car, I said hello to her and she told me that her other half would be out in a few minutes.

Kenny, the better half, came out after her and he, too, was dressed up.

Dark suit, red tie; I kind of didn't get that. Should have been blue, maybe? To match the dress?

No? Whatever.

He got in the car, said the address, and finally, it clicked.

It was Derby Day.

It's one of those days where there's a reason to sport your great clothes and have fun. Never been a big horse racing fan, but I feel like I'm knowledgeable enough in every sport to bullshit my way through a conversation. Some sports I know extremely well, and some I know enough to get by. I could also tell by the gorgeous hat that Kathy was wearing. If I didn't mention it before, her gown was accompanied by a beautiful wide-brimmed hat with a corsage attached to it.

That's a staple for women on Derby Day. The culture started way back when. A hat is considered a significant finishing piece to a woman's outfit. It's like a statement piece although some truly believe that the headdress brings good wishes to betters.

Horse racing, I don't know shit, but I know a little bit about gambling.

So, I tried to talk to Kenny a little bit about the day and he really wasn't having any of it.

They had a short ride, and as we were pulling around the bend to get on the main road, I looked in the mirror and mentioned that they would have a lot of fun and what a great day it was.

"And, if I may say, your hat is awesome. It looks great," I said to Kathy.

Heck, I learned a long time ago, when a woman looks good and spends a lot of time doing herself up, you let her know she looks good. Kathy looked like she had spent a lot of time putting herself together for this day.

Again, the beautiful Ms. Ava is in no trouble at all.

Yet, on the other hand, I do work for tips and mentioning in casual conversation to the woman that she looks good has never hurt the tip jar.

"Thank you. Thank you very much.," Kathy replied. "It's really nice to hear a man acknowledge that a woman has spent time on herself. Isn't it, Kenny?"

Dead silence out of Kenny. Kenny had fucked up, because the tone Kathy used was beyond sarcastic. Kenny had forgotten something.

"Baby, I said you looked good when we were walking down the stairs," Kenny said.

"No. No. No, no, you did not. And you still haven't. Don't consider what you just said to be a makeup, either," Kathy snapped.

And for whatever reason, Kenny decided to shoot me a death look in the mirror as I pulled up in front of the parking lot. A look that could burn through glass, much like Ed's could have.

Tell your woman she looks good when she spends hours fixing herself to go out in public, you stupid ass. What man doesn't understand doing that and how good it makes his woman feel?

I parked and told them to enjoy. "You kids have a good ol' time."

Annnnnnnd they're off.

Q number 52.

DEATH OF A SISTER AND A RIGHT FOOT

Not all situations I've been in are funny or wild, or even comfortable, for that matter.

I remember the time where I picked up Karen and Kari from the airport. Karen's sister had been found dead in her bedroom the night before. They were flying back to Tampa from their vacation and needed to contact family members and make arrangements for the funeral service. Karen had found out just before her flight and, when approaching the car, Kari had to physically help Karen get into the car. She was very weak-kneed and crying hysterically.

Her sister was only 22 years old.

As she called her brother and other family members to inform them, I listened in as she talked to each one, sobbing terribly. Not a fun scenario. I listened for a while—hard not to, small car—and offered information when I could, but not much was going to console Karen, and rightfully so.

"I don't know, they found her lifeless on the floor and that bastard was there, they said for a few hours, and left her," Karen said into the phone to her brother, Max. "I don't know what the bottle said, but the coroner's office said they would get back to me after the toxicology report had been completed," she sobbed.

Seemed like her sister had taken too many pills, according to the coroner's office, and they didn't know whether it was on her own power or with the help of the man she was seeing who was reportedly at the house that night.

"Max, to think that now she's dead at 22. I mean, that's Erin. I want to hug her one last time, and she's gone, oh my God, she's just gone, and we don't know, we just don't know," Karen cried.

Kari sat there consoling her lover, just tearing up at the sight of Karen losing control over the situation.

After driving for a little while, it was nice to see that I could take her mind off of things for a few seconds. After completing her first phone call to her brother, she looked up at where we were on the route I had taken to get to their place, and she was stunned.

"You're a really good driver."

"Thank you," I replied.

"I mean, you got us here pretty quickly."

She had been on the phone a lot during that ride. She didn't know that I wasn't driving any faster than normal. But at that point, Karen would have enjoyed five seconds of normal.

She mentioned to Kari that she was hungry. "Let's order something so it's there pretty close to after we arrive."

"No problem," Kari said. "There's pizza, a sub, pasta, Thai? I know you love Thai food."

Karen nodded and stared blankly out the side window, tears streaming down her face.

Kari looked through her phone and tried to find the place that they had ordered from before. She was disturbed too. You could see that she was feeling the emotions of this horrible experience in her mind and soul.

"How do you spell Thai?" Kari said.

"I don't know?" Karen replied.

Kari smiled for a minute. "C.D.?"

"T-H-A-I," I said, trying to help any way I could.

Kari smiled. "Sorry," she said. Sometimes even the simplest things are so difficult when you're that emotionally distressed.

"No problem," I responded, glad to help.

Karen looked at her and cracked a small smile.

"You can't spell Thai?" she said to her love.

"C.D. has our backs," Kari said.

"Yes, C.D. has been great," Karen agreed.

I won't forget that night as I drove in the dark to the girl's house. Pulling up in front of the driveway, I quickly got out to help with the bags.

"I'm coming right behind you," Kari said to Karen.

"You've been awesome, C.D. I can't thank you enough," Kari said as she looked at me and gave me a half hug.

"Glad I could help, if even for a minute," I said. "Take care of her. God bless you both."

She nodded with a half-smile and ran away down the driveway after Karen to open the door.

Yikes, you feel good for a second, but at the same time, that's nothing you'd wish on anyone.

It wasn't like picking up John and Eve at the airport one night, which brought a challenge I thought I'd never see.

That night was rainy and God-awful. I remember it like it was yesterday.

As I was approaching the end of the terminal to pick them up, they were waving. We had already touched base through the phone and I saw John's bright blue shirt from a mile away. They were right under the sign, and I approached the curbside at about three miles an hour.

There was a white SUV to my left and a man was loading his luggage into it. He looked very rushed and was moving 100 miles an hour. I saw him load his stuff, slam the back door, and move to the passenger's rear door.

He was getting in; I watched him getting in.

But instead, he changed direction and got out.

Dammit.

He pivoted his feet with grace, like a pro basketball star. He was quick. I mean, wow. And as he turned and leaned in, he stepped right under my tire.

The shock or pain on his face, I couldn't tell which one, was vivid.

"Back up, back up!!" he started yelling in my direction.

There were a lot of people, I mean a ton. I could barely hear him amongst all of the chatter and noise at the terminal, and my window was down. He was under my front driver's-side tire, right next to my door, yelling. I could see the hand motions and anguish on his mug.

So, I backed up and put the car in park.

At this point, he was on the ground, looking at the foot like he was counting his toes.

"Are you okay?" I asked him.

He just stared at me, wincing, unable to speak.

"Well, are you okay?" I asked again.

He stepped across my car and grabbed the duffle bag that he'd left on the curb.

That was it. In such a rush, he had left a bag and had gone back for it.

Now, at this point, I didn't know how serious things were. I didn't know how much trouble I was in. I didn't know what would happen next. But before I could blink, he grabbed the bag that was lying on the ground, tossed it into the back of the SUV, and slammed the door. There was no asking again, and frankly, I wasn't going to ask a third time.

I did know this—I had been going about three miles an hour, coming to a dead stop to pick up my couple.

I was looking around, waiting for an aggressive airport cop to come running and say they'd seen the whole thing. Would they take a statement? Arrest me?

Or maybe one of thousands of airport travelers standing there, looking at me with a stink eye, would point me out or blame me.

But there was nothing.

I walked to the back of the car and opened the trunk for John to put in his luggage.

He said, "How are you?" with a huge smile.

"Pretty shaken for a second, to be honest," I responded.

"Why should you be?" Eve asked.

"I don't know. I didn't do anything wrong, so I don't know, but still, I kind of feel that way," I responded.

John and Eve looked ahead from the backseat, ready to roll. They had a calmness to them that I found refreshing.

"Well, that's the guy who was chasing his wife at the airport," John said to Eve.

"Huh?" I asked.

"Yup. He had some big story," he continued. "They left some stuff at home and had to get back to their house. They were arguing at the airport because they were flying standby and the airline only had enough room for one of them. So, he went, and she stayed behind. He was in a ridiculous hurry. Acted like that the whole flight.

"You were almost at a dead stop. You did nothing wrong. He never even stopped to talk to you. Probably because everyone knew it was his fault. We saw the whole thing. We got your back. We're your witnesses. So, has the weather been like this the entire last week?"

I had to chuckle at John's reaction. It wasn't my fault; I didn't feel like it was, and if the man had been really injured, he would still have been lying on the ground, even now.

But, if you have ever been through something like that, it's scary for a few.

Yup, raise your hand if you have been.

Q number 47.

YOU GOT MY WALLET?

Mathieu used to love hanging out at the beach early on Tuesdays and Fridays during the summer. Tuesdays are usually the cheapest flight days for the airlines, and Friday is a popular go-back-to-town day for most businessmen. So, a long time ago, Mathieu started hanging out on the beach behind a row of six major hotels. Including minor ones and little inns, there are about 25-30 hotels within a two-mile stretch. He would sit in the middle of the stretch and wait for a rider. Again, simple science and math were involved. It's a 35-minute trip to the airport, and general time to allow for security and to get to the gate is 90 minutes. Flights start leaving TPA around 6:00 a.m. Roughly two hours off a 6:00 a.m. flight is 3:30 to 4:00 a.m. Massive numbers of business travelers and families who've been vacationing on the beach start calling for rides at that time.

Clearwater is one of the few very recognizable beaches in Florida, very heavily populated with families and travelers, and also a convention center mecca. Lots of businesses hold conferences at the hotels because of the size, scenery, food, entertainment, and large conference halls. Mathieu tipped me off on this just after the summer started, so I frequently pulled up behind his car in a parking spot right on Beach Drive, and we'd celebrate a call with a coffee and a smoke. Never did we make it past 4:00 a.m. without getting a call to the airport.

If you received a call, the object was to drive the 24-mile stretch as fast as possible, dump your rider off at the terminal, and head back to the beach to grab another rider because morning flights at the airport are popular until about 8:00 a.m. Get a second call by 6:00 a.m. and get them into the airport again by 6:45, when arrival flights start to arrive.

So, we would then drive over to the lot and enter the Q, usually at a low number because a lot of general rideshare drivers don't look at this like a business so much as a couple of extra bucks on the side. Sometimes, with tips, we would be sitting with $65-70 at 7:00 a.m., waiting for the first ride out of TPA to start our day. By 2:00-3:00 p.m., we might be sitting on a $150 day and calling it quits to go home and see the kiddos.

On a Friday morning, I picked Mark up really early at a Clearwater hotel. He'd been in Florida spending a few days at a conference, and was flying back home to San Francisco.

"I like your weather here, C.D., and the beaches are beautiful, but it's a little too warm, too humid," Mark said. "Going back home for a little bit cooler air."

He was a quiet guy, but then again, most people don't feel the need to talk your ear off at 4:30 a.m., and thank God for that. He was on the 7:00 a.m. flight out and bragged mildly and quietly about the time he had to get to the airport to make his flight, even telling me about how he was pre-security screen approved and it wouldn't take him long to get to the gate and get his normal morning coffee.

Did someone say coffee? Man, I could use a cup of dark roast with sugar right now. And a donut, frosted chocolate with honey dripping off it, fresh out of the oven. Warm and gooey; maybe two of them.

Sorry.

I dropped off Mark at the blue terminal about 5:30 a.m. and drove back to the lot to get into the Q for my next ride. I entered at 27. Justin and I had just finished coffee and a smoke when I got another ride out of the airport. It was three young women coming home from vacation in Texas, going back to their home in St. Petersburg. They didn't say much, either; must have been in the air that day. But I'll drive anyone, that's fine. About halfway through the 30-minute ride, my cell phone rang. It sits clipped to the front air-conditioner vent in a holster that the beautiful Ms. Ava bought for me to better see the GPS system and to connect the charger more easily.

Now, I have a policy that I never answer the phone in the middle of a ride. Some say that's okay; you can answer it. I just never really feel comfortable driving with people in the car, on a job, and talking to another person about anything.

It can wait, whatever it is. But the same number called again. And again.

And again.

Finally, on the street in St. Petersburg, where the women lived, I decided to call the number back. It was, of course, San Francisco Mark.

Uhh oh.

"I left my wallet in your car," was the first thing I heard from him.

"Ladies?" I asked quickly before they got out. "Does one of you happen to be sitting on a wallet?"

"I am," a young woman responded.

Shit.

"Do you have it?" Mark asked.

"Yes, I do. I'm headed back to the airport now with it. But it's going to take me at least 30 minutes to get back to you."

Looking at the clock, it was now 6:40 a.m.

That 7:00 a.m. flight was in serious jeopardy.

"Shit. Okay, well, I really need it. It has everything inside of it. I couldn't get through security. Everything I own is inside it. I'll be waiting for you at the same place you dropped me off. Please bring it?"

Of course I was going to bring it. It was his wallet.

As I pulled up in front of the terminal 23 minutes later, Mark was standing there, rushed.

"They're holding the flight for me," he said.

"Go, run. Get out of here," I replied.

Mark handed me a $20 bill and ran like hell back between the sliding glass doors of the blue terminal.

Twenty dollars wasn't bad for coming back and doing something nice for someone who'd messed up.

He was a nice man, whom I wish well.

I hope he caught that flight because they only run direct across the country early in the morning once a day.

Q number 44.

FIVE-STAR COMMENTS

I can tell you this, I think it says a lot when a person takes extra time to leave a note about a car ride. You can play along at home and guess as to which rides a few of these go to.

Here are some of the five star comments I have received from the riders over my time.

- "Awesome guy, very friendly and professional. Highly recommend." March 17

- "By far the BEST driver I have EVER had!!!! You were so amazing. I can't thank you enough!!" July 17

- "Fantastic and friendly. Got us where we were going fast and even spun back around to return my girlfriend's cell phone she left in the car. Thanks, C.D." May 17

- "All-around awesome! Felt comfortable and well taken care of." November 17

- "Thanks so much for making our morning trip to the airport smooth. It was nice chatting with you and I was surprised when I heard you also took my sister-in-law to Tampa!" July 17

- "Good luck to the Sox!" May 17

- "In three years, the best driver I have ever had." June 17

- "Absolute legend! Thanks." June 17

- "Thanks so much for the advice!!" July 17

- "Very nice." May 17

- "Thank you!" May 17

- "Great guy, excellent service. Go Pats!" May 17

- "Thanks for the easy ride and good convo." May 17

- "Much appreciated!" May 17

- "Excellent driving and great personality!" May 17

- "Good recommendations on places to visit." June 17

- "Thank you so much." June 17

- "C.D. was awesome!" June 17

- "Thanks, C.D.! Nice talking with you." July 17

- "Very professional." July 17

- "Thank you for prompt service!" July 17

- "Great job helping me find a good spot for dinner as well as getting me to my destination efficiently." July 17

- "Great service." July 17

- "Great guy! Funny and very responsive!" August 17

- "Great ride!" August 17

- "Awesome!" September 17

- "Thanks!!" December 17

- "A pleasure." April 17

- "Most excellent!" April 17

Getting lower. Q number 43.

DEAD KEY FOB

I've driven people to work, home, and to sporting events. I've also driven people to concerts, seminars, and out to dinner.

Bob was a whole different type of ride. I still smile about him today. He was a tough-looking man. A rough exterior, scratchy beard, slightly spiked blond hair, and stoic personality. But it seemed to be a normal ride to his home in Brandon, FL, until I found out it wasn't normal at all.

My job as a driver is to drive you where you want to go and follow what directions you give me, within reason and subject to my personal judgement.

For whatever reason, one person I picked up actually said, "Are you okay with taking me to my home?"

Uhhh, yeah.

On this night, Bob said he wanted to go home, so I took him there. But there was more to this than just a ride, and he could have just told me, because it ended up being a really good laugh about something pretty silly and actually common.

But not to Bob.

For most of the ride to his house, Bob was an anything-but-normal late forties-early fifties man who had flown in from business and wanted to lie down on his soft bed after a long taxing trip. He seemed edgy, grumpy, and annoyed as we cruised the highway. We talked about, well, not very much. He flipped through a gun magazine and stared ahead quietly, mentioning the weather and the usual stuff with a low deep tone to his voice. It rained pretty hard that night and traffic was slow and congested, yet when we pulled up in front of his house, everything still seemed pretty normal. The rain had even stopped completely, which was kind of eerie, until he looked at me with a blank stare.

"Okay, C.D., when we stop, I just need you to stay here for a few minutes," he said. "Please don't get out of the car, just stay right here."

"Here, Bob?"

"Yes," he said.

Okay, I thought to myself, *he wants to tip me and has cash in the house. No problem. That's nice of him. Finally, someone who has a head on his shoulders.* And then, it dawned on me that he'd never asked for his bags and he was walking around the back of the house, not entering the front door. His two suitcases were still in my trunk, and he had gone inside the house.

Stay here. This was one moment in time that I wasn't tapping on the steering wheel and listening to the beat. I was panicking.

What had I done to piss this guy off? This had to be something major.

He'd left his stuff and gone inside his house. I couldn't even run; I had his luggage.

He's going to come back and shoot me.

Nahhh, WTF are you thinking?

But seriously, this guy, he's a drug dealer and he's making a sale. Eight-balls all around. This really isn't his house, I'm aiding and abetting. Fuck, I'm done. I'm going to jail and I'm going to end up someone's bitch. Mathieu will never let me hear the end of this. But then again, if I do end up someone's bitch, he and Branson may be prouder of me than ever.

I noticed Bob exiting the front door and heading toward the car, but not the same way he'd entered.

Here he comes. Shhhh, don't say anything. Okay, here we go.

Bob slowly headed down the walkway, opened the door, and climbed back into the car.

"C.D?" he said.

"Uhhhh, yeah, Bob," I said with a lump in my throat like a frog on a Sunday morning after having a major cold the night before. All that phlegm floating around in your throat—gross. Wait, wrong chapter.

Wait. Raise your hand if you've ever had that phlegm.

Ever had one of those mornings? That phlegm is gross.

"Okay, take me back to the airport, please, C.D."

Back to the airport? Wait, did we complete the drug deal? I wonder if the guy has an off-shore bank account? All the cool drug dealers have an off-shore bank account. I don't think the best thing to do is take him to the airport. He can escape, fly in, make the deal, and fly out, bam.

Or maybe he's going back to the airport so he can harm all those people, too? No way. Not without an excuse. I've got to ask.

"Bob?" I asked.

"Yeah, C.D., the airport?"

"Yeah, I'm headed that way, but honestly, what gives?"

"I'd rather not say, so can we just leave it at that?" he said.

Shit. I knew he wouldn't tell me a word. He's keeping me safe because he can't tell me anything so I'm not an accessory.

Tampa Airport is doomed. What have I done? I picked up a psychopath rider who has a plan to destroy all mankind.

Okay, maybe not, but I still have to save the world.

So, I stared at him in the mirror for a few minutes, almost like a game of chicken, until he gave up his motive. I had to know what this entailed so I could save the world.

"Okay," he finally said. "I got to the airport and got off the plane."

And called me to take you to the drug deal?

"I had driven my car to long-term parking and parked it there during my stay," he continued.

Probably a bomb in the car to blow up long-term parking lot. Jesus, we're all doomed. Mathieu, El Presidente, Jax, Branson, Justin, Howard—well, Howard, never mind—don't come this way, you are doomed; doomed, I say.

"I was only gone a few days," he said. "I went to the parking lot before I called you and tried to start it, but when I pointed the key fob at the car, it was dead."

"OMG, that's hideous. I can't take it. I can't believe you, you—wait, you had a dead car key fob?" I asked.

"Yep, so I basically rented you to take me home so I could go upstairs and get my spare one. The car is entirely keyless entry and I need the clicker," he explained.

"Well, wait, so, umm, why didn't we just go to a supermarket or a store to get a few batteries and replace them?" I asked.

I mean, so sorry to bring logic into all of this, but hey, at least now I knew I wasn't going to die, nor were millions of others at the airport, so we could examine this and find out why we didn't just drive two miles instead of all the way home, then have to come all the way back.

"Oh. Now that you say that, I never considered it," he said. "I was too embarrassed to bring the whole situation up. I felt stupid. I just wanted to quietly go home and get what I needed so I could get back and go home and go to bed. Man, I'm tired."

Never considered that. Just considered not telling you and scaring the holy hell out of you for 90 minutes.

I felt stupid too, or as Justin says, retarded, thinking I was in any danger. But it's fun to be scared sometimes, no?

Q number 39.

COCAINE AND EGGS

As we have seen over my experiences, being scared can be fun, and can also be downright intimating.

Odd, with a side of uncomfortable, can be explained as driving around with Manny.

I picked Manny up early one morning, 3:30, outside of the casino. Instead of heading straight to the airport, I used to live around the corner from the casino, so I figured I'd try it. Yes, I know it's against most that I preach with science and my old man's rule of thumb, but heck, it's only one ride before I head to the lot. It can't be all that bad, can it?

It seemed like a good idea at the time. You could tell the riffraff had just been let out when I headed up the casino way. There were drunk people stumbling out the front door and chatting, many of them looking for rides.

Manny was standing out at the pickup line, waving his hands frantically, when I pulled around the corner at this massive entrance. He was dressed up in a white nylon sweat suit, black sneakers, and a short blond haircut spiked up with mousse.

He opened the door like he was going to tear it off from the hinges, and he was not a big person by any means. He looked average in height and weight as he got into the car really fast and talked even faster. I felt like it wasn't a good idea to ever take off my seatbelt around Manny; everything was fast. He got into the car and announced probably the one thing you don't want to announce, since you risk getting bashed in the head:

He told me he had won about $2500 at the casino overnight and was in the mood for breakfast. I wasn't sure if I believed him or not. He had a tone to him that was believable, yet he looked completely full of shit.

"Where you from, Tampa?" he asked.

"No, Boston. Been here for the last nine years," I responded proudly.

"Oh, no shit; you're my boy. I'm from Rhode Island."

Technically he was and he wasn't. He was a Rhode Island guy, but he was close enough and definitely New England, so I guess he qualified as my boy.

But what he'd do later on in the car ride immediately disqualified him from ever being my boy.

"How about them Sox, huh?" he asked. "They come down here and kick the ever-loving shit out of this shit team in this shit stadium. I love it."

Manny was much different then Kevin because he was a transplant like me, freshly moved down here, yet mentally still stuck in the Northeast as a sports fan.

"So, you like the Sox, right? I mean, how can you not?" Manny asked.

"Of course I do," I replied.

"That's worth a $20," he said, and dropped a $20 bill in the cup holder between my two seats.

"And, of course, the Pats?" he said. "I mean, come on, Brady is the friggin' GOAT, ya know. Word."

"Heck yes," I said as Manny dropped another $20 in the cup holder. This was getting good. I knew my two next answers and I was going to be up to $80 by the time it was over. Maybe Manny had hit it big in the casino after all, because he certainly didn't look concerned dropping twenties in my holder and I wasn't answering questions of a high degree of difficulty.

At times, Manny paused between talking, and I just hoped he hadn't had too much to drink and I was going to pay the ultimate price of spending my newly acquired $80 to get my carpets and seats cleaned. He remained under control, though, as we traveled the highway and headed downtown to his destination. Manny rubbed his chest quite often and it took a minute before I understood what he was doing. He was looking for his smokes.

"So, can we smoke in here?" he asked.

"No," I said. "I'm headed to the airport after this for a full day's work and I don't want my car smelling like smoke. Riders hate that."

"Oh yeah? Who's your next ride?" Manny asked. "And at what time?"

I didn't have another ride yet, but I was headed to the airport to start my day and get in line, just like every other morning.

"Come on. Who's your next ride, and more importantly, how much is your next fare total going to be?" he asked.

I didn't know. That's a crapshoot. It could be a good one or an excellent one, so what could I tell this guy?

"I have a regular I need to pick up at 6:00 a.m., going to Sarasota. It will cost about $200."

A regular is a rider that you get to know or give really good service to and they ask for your phone number and let you know when they need another ride. I have a few regulars, but make no mistake about it, I didn't have a regular ride at 6:00 a.m. The airport to Sarasota was not $200, but I knew what Manny was getting at and was interested to see how deep his pockets were and what his next move would be.

Jackpot.

"Okay, here's $300 and we go get breakfast and hang out," he said as he turned the wad of cash he had backward and started to count 100-dollar bills. "Skip the ride to Sarasota; too fucking far to drive anyway." He placed the money in the coffee holder.

Did Manny play for the same team as Branson and Mathieu and want to spend quality time with me? I have Ava at home and I don't play for that team, no matter how many twenties you stuff that cup holder with, but $300 was a good hit from my boy if we were going to just hang out and have breakfast.

Something just didn't sound right though; something was odd, just didn't add up.

"Fuck, we're going out for breakfast, I just made that decision. Seriously, you pick the spot," he said. "I'm okay with wherever, but we got to do a line of cocaine first. It definitely makes the eggs taste better."

There it was.

That was the glue to make me pull the car over immediately and politely ask Manny to get out.

"Really?" Manny said as he opened the door. "You're a stupid nigga boy, you know that?"

"Dude, we're both white," I responded. "And that's all the white we got going on here; keep your powder."

Goodbye, Manny.

As I arrived at the lot, Mathieu was in his car. He sat there, bug-eyed, listening to the story and laughing.

"I have one question," he said. I knew what was coming from a mile away.

"How was the coke?" he smirked.

I started to shake my head.

"Oh, God," Mathieu yelled, and beeped his horn.

Q number 36.

LEVEL 42

An old management boss and really good friend of mine used to always say, "Otto, you have the right to say whatever you want. You also have the right to get punched right in the mouth after you say it."

That was what we called the secret agent 7219 twist on the First Amendment.

For what it's worth, I hope I never reach that status in the car toward a rider standing on the dangerous side of the fence. Manny has probably been the closest in enticing a square-off.

I always used to nod my head in agreement after my boss said it because that's what has always made this country great; it's also been one root for my humor.

Anybody has the right to say whatever they want at any moment. For the most part, I usually do, and as he used to say on top of that, "and you might run into that one motherfucker who doesn't like what you have to say and reaches back and punches you right in the grill after you say it." Well, come on; with my size, I'm never really worried about that. I mean, if you feel frisky and you want to jump, jump. Being an ex-bouncer, I do, as you have seen a little, like to push the envelope a tad.

Well said, jefe. I miss seeing you on a regular basis every day. It was a true honor to work with you, to share all the laughs that we did, and I learned so much from you. You even taught me to deliver my arrogant humor through the world of corporate email chains as long as I ended things with a smiley face.

"Don't forget the smiley face," he'd say. "It's an email that's telling you off but the smiley face leaves doubt, like, did he just say that? Ohh, we good."

He had a high-pitched shriek in his delivery that was able to grab the room; I've stolen it a time or two hundred, I have to confess, but we mimic the greats as a show of appreciation and tribute. Copying is truly the greatest form of flattery. His other signature was the roll of eyes upward, to the right, and a long pause after you said something he knew was fucked up and needed to wait and give ample time before he blasted you. You could see the eyes go up to the right and pause over his glasses that used to slide down his face at times. And if you couldn't see it and had said something super stupid, he would remove the glasses to show the rise. Absolutely classic, but it needs to be delivered correctly.

Raise your hand—you know what I'm talking about; hopefully you've done it, not seen it from others. That would mean you're the one saying stupid shit.

It's funny, most of the time you naturally want to thank your parents for their nurturing and for teaching you right and wrong. And for the most part, I do; I thank them a ton. But in getting older, I've figured out for myself that they're just as full of shit as anyone else.

As you grow, you encounter some people in your life, maybe only one or two of them, that you learn so much from that you can consider it a blessing. It may be a coach, a workmate, or boss that you encounter who changes your life for the negative and makes you not want to go that road, or a huge positive and you cherish it. Two of my ex-bosses from the environmental world in Tampa are my boys and I will be forever grateful for all the lessons they taught me, the sarcasm and wisdom and the overall balance of when to say what, and more importantly sometimes, when not to say what. One, as I mentioned before, is up in Virginia and we still remain close. The other has disappeared into retirement; haven't seen him in years, but I'm certain he still rules with his iron fist slamming down on his desk while he yells out, "I'm talking!" He hated to be interrupted, always feeling someone would steal his thunder before he could get it out, and therefore you also knew when he was talking.

"You and I aren't from the same parts of the country, but we understand how to hustle, make things happen, and motherfucker next," he'd say.

First time he said it, I was confused, thinking he was telling me to get out of his office and he was moving on to someone else. He clearly was not. He was explaining to me that we had been brought up the same way in terms of a work ethic: do it, get it done, out of the way, motherfucker next. I kind of relate it to a great punchline, like a ball player raising his finger as the shot is in midair, knowing it's going to directly hit its target.

AGM Alpha, not so much. There's nothing good I want to ever emulate in my life concerning that man. He was a little troll who had been affected by a severe case of Napoleon syndrome and was never going to recover. At times, we would imagine running the bus over him and then putting it in reverse and backing up over him again if we ever saw him crossing the street. He used his AGM title in every way he could to be the biggest tyrant possible. Some day he will meet up with the wrong person in the proverbial dark alley and well, hopefully that person runs over him a third time and leaves the crime scene.

Raise your hand if you know someone like that, either the good leader or the evil dictator.

Another fragment of my humor has always been: may the bridges I burn light the way. It's not always the correct approach, and I have gotten a few uneasy looks over my lifetime, but I will take shit for a while to have the laugh or to get the joke out. Punchlines, deliveries, shots, as my old workers used to call them, are funny, but not all people find them humorous, especially if they're at the bottom of the punchline. As I mentioned earlier, an old boss, Davis, used to say to me, "Otto, you are the person who says stuff that everyone is thinking during that quiet moment, but no one has the balls to say."

I enjoy that moment. I used to make Davis walk away redder than an apple. I wasn't ever sure if it was my tone, delivery, or the sauce that was his poison.

Great man. May he rest in peace.

Now, it could be my size which makes those punchlines easier to deliver, or fuck it, someone has to say it; may as well be me.

Have you ever had something funny to say and held it in and bitten your tongue and not said it given, maybe, the fragile ego of a person? Sure you have.

I don't play nice. I usually piss people off when I deliver the line. So the older I get, I have learned more and more to hold back.

I guess I'm learning to enjoy laughter more internally than publicly. When I was younger, I had a ton to say. I was young, big, and thought I was hilarious. I once told a good friend of my family's, while he was complaining about the bathroom situation with his six children, all girls, that if someone had ever bothered to take him to a drugstore and buy him a box of condoms, he would be able to spend a lot more time in that very bathroom. Carl ended up throwing a handheld scanner at me because I guess I pinched a nerve with that one.

I still bring moments of jackassery to the game in my older age, just not as often. The fabulous Ms. Ava says it's more my looks and reactions to people's comments and situations that make her laugh. Yet people who really know me well know that if I'm being quiet, it's for a damn good reason.

I once had a boss back in Boston who was ex-military. He would say funny stuff at times, but I never wanted to give him the upper edge, so I never laughed at anything he said. I would give him a stoic look, acting like an English guardsman, showing no emotion, even though sometimes he was absolutely hilarious. Cheers, Truco.

I miss my buddy Rob, in Michigan, as well. He had more sarcasm than I could imagine. He was very funny and didn't have to say very much. He had a look that could tell you how many different ways you were legitimately stupid and he wouldn't have to say a word. He was a prick at times, but a funny prick.

Rob and I were customer service managers for the longest time in a trucking company. His claims to fame were in the bathroom. He used to sit down and go to the bathroom and his phone would ring. He always used to yell out loud in the stall when it rang, "Jesus Christ, I can't even take a good shit without someone having an issue."

Rob and I shared a lot of the same smirks. I miss you too, Rob. I hope you're well.

Greg had a delivery with humor and one-liners that was about as funny as I've ever heard. He and I had great chemistry in telling jokes and finishing stories and unleashing tirades on people in weak moments. No one was safe. Our game was usually ping-ponging people back and forth between the two of us until you were mentally tired and couldn't hang anymore, especially Sammy, our front desk receptionist. We used to torment her many times per day. She took it well and had a great sense of humor.

"Assholes," she used to call us in a deep southern twang.

We all laughed together in the end, and God, did it make the day go by quicker.

Q number 32.

SHELLIE'S SNACK, PT. 2

As we pulled in front of the loudspeaker, I greeted the man and announced Shellie's order of a 20-piece chicken and four cheeseburgers. We paid the $17.34 tab and pulled away from the lines of the drive-thru when I thought, *yeah, I gotta ask.*

"It was really nice of you to get a 20-piece chicken and four cheeseburgers to bring to the party. Is everybody bringing something?" I ask.

All along, I was praying, *please don't spill any crumbs or a drop of liquid in the car; I don't feel like cleaning today or any day, for that matter.* She hadn't stopped eating since I'd handed her the large fast food bag. Don't get me wrong, I like to eat, but holy shit. This was impressive.

She looked out the side window for a good few minutes, then faded back to me and sighs. I didn't know whether she was full or pissed.

"No, this is my snack before I get to the party," she said to me.

Wow. A snack? Even if you don't think you're going to like the food at the party, that's a hell of a snack to pound down before arriving. That would make most people sick.

Shellie ate every bite that day in the car on the sunny ride to her uncle's. I didn't know what to say to her. Again, that's very unusual for me.

I didn't know if this was a funny moment, where she was just an absolute pig who couldn't stop eating, she didn't plan on eating at the party or for a few days after that, or she'd found 45 minutes with nothing to do but eat, so she was going to.

Or was it maybe deep dark childhood moments or one truly horrible experience in life which had led her to sometimes just gorging herself?

Raise your hand if you could even dream of eating a 20-piece chicken and four cheeseburgers in one sitting.

Mathieu always used to say, "Be kind to the inner fat kid."

Scary. Punt on this one. Wait for a turnover and get them on the next possession.

Q number 31.

A KNIFE, BUT NOT FOR TURKEY

Scary would be one most memorable time back in Boston that I will never ever forget.

I remember that day even though it was forever ago. It seems like forever ago, but I remember it like it was yesterday.

Working in the snow and cold, I hated it. Yuck, that's what dragged me to Tampa to begin with. The weather during the winter up north was a most unpleasurable experience.

It really was a great city to live in; tons of history, culture, and good times.

Raise your hand if you've been to Boston. Yeah, most of you know what I'm talking about.

I was working for a small parcel company. I made good money at the time and the job was fun, kind of like my job now. We got to wear shorts every day and at times we were the demented delivery guys who wore shorts year-round and had contests to see who could go all year long without putting on pants.

The windburns on our legs in winter would sometimes be really bothersome.

I almost wrote a book back then when I worked for that company, about the lives and times of delivery drivers.

I had a title picked out for it and everything. *25 and Out*. You see, you needed 25 years to retire with a union pension back then. So, I was going to work 25 years and I was out.

I was going to tell various stories, similar to this book, surrounding my daily deliveries and pickups. Most of the experiences were funny, and a few of them very extreme.

I only made it 11 years with the company. After relocating to the Midwest, the company didn't have room for me and I was out before my 25 years were up.

Time goes by, things go really fast, and now I'm writing this book, so I guess it was always destiny for me to be an author. Now, I'm going to tell a story that would have made the old book.

One of the scary, but very good ones.

It was back a bit ago. I believe it was the fall of 1997 and it was Thanksgiving week.

I really enjoyed my job; come to think of it, I've always enjoyed my jobs. I was always told how lucky I was because I never minded getting up for work in the morning.

I always liked what I did at this gig and I was working second shift at the time. I drove a step van most days and did small package pickups and deliveries. I worked mostly north of Boston, but there were a few years I worked deep in the heart, downtown.

I was out late and was trying to get rid of everything I had left in the back. I had a few deliveries left that I had moved up to the front seat and was trying to go back to the home base with an empty van. It was just starting to snow. The weather had been turning for a few days and it had that feel.

Winter was coming; it was getting much darker earlier in the day. Darkness started at about 4:00 p.m., and I was driving in a small city, deep in the heart of Boston, at about 6:15 p.m. I had one more package I wanted to try to get rid of, so I pulled up in front of Howland St. and put the van in park. It was a triple-decker house. Triple-decker houses were famous on this side of town, but I could tell it wasn't taken care of very well. For one, the siding was peeling off. The bad weather looked like it had taken a toll. Another thing was that the first- and third-floor apartments didn't have lights on outside the doors and the street light above the driveway wasn't on.

I never thought twice about it, though. I was ready to grab the small cylinder I had and head up to the third floor to get rid of the thing.

"C.D., where are you?" the CB radio spoke just as I was getting ready to exit the van.

"Hey Jimmy, I'm going to do this one on Howland and then return," I told him as I leaned back in to answer.

Jimmy was my dispatch for the company. I received all of my calls from him when I was supposed to pick stuff up. If I had an issue delivering something, I'd call Jimmy. We had two-way phones at the time, but all vans were equipped with two-way radios that we used.

"Get that one done and get on back here," Jimmy said. "It's Thanksgiving, man; let's go."

It wasn't Thursday, but I sure knew what he meant. It was the Wednesday before and I was ready for the four-day break coming up, looking forward to doing a little relaxing and turkey eating.

So, I grabbed the cylinder and headed up the stairs. I was looking for Sheila. She was on the third floor, so I started to jog up the steps at a good pace.

I got to the top of the stairs and found a screen door covering a hardwood door. I opened it and rapped on the hardwood a couple of times.

The first thing I noticed was that the porch was not very big and it was all screened in. Maybe two or three people could stand on this porch at the most. Put a BBQ grill on the porch and you were down one person, maybe two if you had smaller people standing on it. It was definitely not a space for grilling or chilling out with multiple people. I could smoke a cigarette on this porch and that was about it.

No one's answering; let's try knocking again.

God, it was getting chilly out. The wind was picking up and chafing my legs, but of course it was whipping harder because I was noticeably 40-50 feet up on this rickety stairwell. Of course, I had on shorts because we were early into the winter season, but I honestly hadn't expected to be out this late.

Bang, bang, bang.

I wasn't seeing any signs of life out of this apartment. Maybe it was vacant, or maybe they'd gone away for vacation.

Maybe I was crazy for standing here.

I could leave it and run. We had a rule where if an area was safe, we could leave the package and mark LDFD on the paperwork. LDFD was an acronym for left door, front door. This place, the more I looked around, was not safe. I mean, it was on the third floor, and nobody was going to come up unless they lived here, yet as I looked around, I just didn't see it as safe.

Raise your hand if you think we should leave it.

Fuck it, I'm going to try one more time and if I don't see life, I'm gone.

Wait, hold on. Here we go. It looks like someone is home.

I noticed a body in the window and a small light came on inside the house. The door handle started to turn, the door creaking open so slowly I thought it was jammed or broken.

Yes, this was my freedom, my chance to give this package away, sign on line 47, and roll.

Here was my moment.

"What do you want?" a voice sternly demanded as the door reached halfway open. I could see a man, a pretty big dude.

Wait, I'm a pretty big dude, but this was a pretty big dude.

"I'm looking for Sheila, please. I have a delivery for her. Why are you yelling?" I asked.

"Do I look like a fucking Sheila to you?" said the African-American man with a white T-shirt and dark pants, getting closer to me and rivaling me in size. He was still inside the doorway with the screen door shut, but I could now see very clearly that he had a kitchen knife in his left hand, probably a good 12- to 16-inch knife.

The shine of the knife as he twisted it ever so slowly in his hand gleamed in the bad lighting.

Goddamn, LDFD looks good right now.

But I'm 100 percent sure right now, this is not a safe place, for more reasons than one.

My eyes never left the knife now that it was in plain view.

"No. No, you don't look like a fucking Sheila to me." I slowly started to step back and felt my way with my right foot for the top stair. I was planning on easing myself backward and slowly proceeding down the steps.

"Then go the fuck on and get to somewhere else," he said, opening the screen door. At this point, I was fully aware that the screen door was no match for the knife he held, in case he decided to jab at me, so I needed to be quick but smooth.

I can't tell you how tense those short five minutes were. I'm a big dude. Throw all of that out the window when it's an uneven confrontation and I'm on the short end of the weapon side to represent myself. I was not going to wish this man a happy holiday or a happy Thanksgiving. I was going to slowly get the fuck out of here, like he so kindly suggested, yet I was going to do it with my limbs attached to my torso and my future still left to live, not flashing so quickly before my eyes like it was.

I slowly made my way back down the first few stairs in a backward-stepping motion until I knew I was far enough to turn around. I didn't want my back toward the man and, to be honest, the stairs were so thin, there wasn't a hell of a lot of room to turn around. But mostly, I didn't want my back turned toward that person. He never moved out of the doorway, as far as I could see. When I got to the second floor, I quickly turned around and bolted as gracefully as a man of my size can down the stairs and headed for the van.

When I got in the van, I slowly turned the ignition as I locked the door.

Okay. I was okay. There were no thoughts in my head. No words spoken for quite a bit.

No situation where he followed me down the stairs and confronted me again.

Thankfully, no situation where, as I enjoyed my first moments of peace and safety, there was a bang on the window like a horror movie where a killer reappeared and scared the shit out of me in an attempt to finish his business.

I pulled the column down into drive, stepped on the gas, turned my directional on, and cruised out of the parking lot in front of the triplex.

It was a good few minutes before I contacted Jimmy about being in the truck and headed back toward the depot.

My heart was still in my throat but I managed to get out a few words while pressing the mic as I put it close to my lips.

"322, clear, coming in," I said.

"Good to hear your voice. Come on in," Jimmy said, with his usual friendly and comforting voice.

"Glad to be heard." Jesus Christ, was it ever.

Later, upon returning to the depot, I told my story to some of the drivers and Jimmy.

Jimmy asked me if I wanted to file a report and have the address investigated.

I declined. I was okay with leaving it alone and didn't really want to go back there in my head.

A few of the guys suggested that, whoever my match was that night, he probably thought I was a cop and I was potentially showing up for a drug raid. I had the stature of a decent-sized police officer and package delivery drivers are commonly used in situations like that for a drug raid.

I never want to know what was in that package. I never want to know who Sheila was, and I still don't to this day. Or know who that man is or was.

I'm good.

Q is moving slowly today, but that's okay. I'm having fun. I hope you are, too.

Q number 28.

I HAVE KEYS; I NEVER LEFT THEM

On a crisp early morning in December, I was working the airport when I got a call from Paula at the blue terminal. Funnily enough, after I texted, she texted me back and told me she was at the blue departures side. That was actually a smart move because it was a very busy morning and people do that from time to time. People will head up to the departures side so when a driver comes to pick them up, they're usually the only ones looking to get out, when every other person is looking to get dropped off and checked in. Also, the departures side is usually not as busy, so it's easy to find someone.

I had to hand it to Paula, but things changed a little when I pulled up to the terminal.

Paula was about 5'4", red-haired, and an attractive woman, but the thing that stood out the most about her was that she was dressed in a flight attendant uniform. We· would get them every now and again, going home after their shift and after talking to the guys in the lot; most of them said that was an attendant thing to do. They would go upstairs to the departures area to be picked up because they didn't want to deal with the massive number of people downstairs.

Kudos to Paula.

"Hey, C.D., how are you? I'm going to St. Petersburg," her bubbly voice said as she sat down in the backseat.

"Okay, on the way," I replied as I cruised out of the terminal and into the bright Florida sunshine on my way out of the airport.

"Where did you come in from?" I asked.

"Toronto," she said.

"Brrrrrr," I responded as an actual shiver went through my bones. I remembered the days of that cold up north. And it was December, so I was sure she'd come from the real cold.

"Okay, so, well, actually, Phoenix, through Dallas and Toronto, and now here for a little bit."

"Nice," I responded. *I really didn't care to know all of your pit stops, all the cities you've been in on a 36-hour stint, but okay.*

"Going to see parents? Family? Husband?" I asked.

"My boyfriend," she said. "I haven't seen him in about a month and he doesn't know I'm coming. So, the second I got a break, I figured I'd head down here and hang out."

"Oh, that's nice," I said, thinking to myself, *this may have potential if he doesn't know you're coming.*

Throughout the trip to St. Petersburg, Paula talked about her boyfriend, Rick. He had a condo in a high rise by the water on the beach. She was originally from Dallas and liked it here a lot better but was waiting for a transfer to come in so she could be based out of Tampa. Rick was a financial planner and they had been together for about a year. Things sounded great between them. They sounded like a happy couple that you cheer for, or at least that was my opinion of the story as I heard it through Paula's eyes.

Not too long after we started talking, Paula's phone rang.

"Oh," she says, "it's Rick now. Hey, babe."

I just stared ahead at the road, a little bummed because I had to turn my radio down a bit for her to talk on the phone. That was a common courtesy practice that we all discussed back at the lot some time ago. Justin even goes so far ask to ask riders what music they like to listen to.

I don't.

You get what I like to listen to; sometimes sports radio, classical music, and sometimes general pop. And don't play with my windows; that drives me nuts. Usually, I have the child lock on them so you can't mess with them. I hate that.

"I had some time off coming to me," Paula said.

Uh oh, he's going to find out she's here. Maybe everything will be okay. I hate to be pessimistic, but it never turns out good. Every story I get in the car when a bad or weird plot twist is headed my way, I usually run over it like a speed bump, hard and rough.

It's never the happy-go-lucky moment that everyone thinks. The end of the movie comes, the happy music plays, and the bright light comes on, and everyone always lives safely at the end. Nope.

In my car, the plane crashes, the building blows up at the end, and everyone dies. No one lives and it's a catastrophic ending.

Here we go.

"So, I had some time off and I'm in Tampa, honey; well, St. Petersburg, actually, headed to the condo. Your condo. Well, I told you last week I might have the time, so I called my dad and asked him if he would watch the dogs, and he said no problem. 20 minutes or so. Hey C.D., how long before we get to the place?"

"23 minutes," I responded, looking at the GPS.

"23 minutes," she told Rick. I fly back Sunday. Come to your work? Why? Who cares if the condo is dirty; I'll clean it. I don't mind. I don't want to come to your work. I want to unpack and shower and rest up a bit. I've been traveling for the last two days. What time are you coming home? It's 8:30 a.m. now. What do you mean how am I going to get in? I have my keys; I never left them. Well, you don't have to be rude about it. What's wrong with the condo? And don't give me a line about it's a mess. Don't you have to stay at work? Babe, I don't need you to come home and meet me, I'm fine."

The ending credits are near. I hear the plane going down into a big lake, maybe a fiery crash.

Let's see, raise your hand if you think that another woman is now in Rick's condo and it just happens he doesn't want Paula to see because, well, she thinks Rick is only hers.

Now raise your hand if you think the woman is still in the condo at this time and is trying to get out before we get there and Paula is going to bump smack into her upon arrival.

I vote B.

"What's going on, Rick? Start talking. What do you mean don't go? You aren't making any sense at all. Well, we're pulling into the entrance now. Are you kidding me? We're a few buildings away. Number three, C.D, just pull up in front. No, I'm serious, babe. I'm here in front of the place now. C.D. is going to get my bag and I'm going to go upstairs, whether you like it or not. What!?"

That didn't sound good.

"He wants to talk to you," she said.

Me. Me? What do I have to do with this whole scenario, please tell me? Anyone?

"Hello?" I said as Paula handed me her phone.

"Dude, she cannot go into that friggin' condo. Pull away, do whatever you have to do, but she can't go in there," this voice said.

I can't stop her. I don't want to stop her. I'm out of this.

"Listen, buddy, I'm parked, my trunk is open, and your lady is getting her bag out of the trunk," I explained. And then I thought to myself, and swished the gasoline can around a little bit.

"Or *one* of your ladies is getting her bag out of my trunk," I corrected myself. "Sorry, brother, you're hanging with the hardcore now."

Just as I finished my sentence, I shut the phone and handed it back to Paula. Yeah, it was an actual flip phone; I couldn't believe it. Hadn't seen one of those in years.

"I'm going in," she said to me.

"Okay, it's not my call," I responded. "But it might not be good when you get up there. Did you just hear that?"

"Yes. It is what it is." She stared back at me.

Paula proceeded to roll her bag toward the elevator in the main garage area. She stood there, waiting for a bell.

Kind of like the ping starting to go off on my app.

Judy was looking to be picked up a few blocks away, 2.7 miles away, to be exact.

As I pulled away from the complex, I saw Paula go into the open elevator doors and it was like she disappeared.

Sometimes you don't hear the end of the stories and you wonder how they turned out. Sometimes you don't wonder how they turned out, but hope the people are okay.

I feared more for Rick that day as I pulled away than I did for Paula.

Paula was going to be just fine. It might sting for a while, but I had the feeling that she would be just fine.

Q number 25.

SO, I'M LIKE, OKAY

"It hit it!" I yelled from the other side of the parking lot.

"It fucking didn't. OMG, are you blind?" Justin replied.

"Listen, I'm standing right here and boom, it hit it. Thank you."

Jax nodded his head. "Yeah, I got to go with that. Good one, C.D."

"Two blind drivers," Justin said. "How do they let you drive at all? You guys are like retarded, not like retarded, but retarded."

It was Tuesday morning, 6:15, overcast skies and a tad breezy, and we were playing our normal game of Flick the Cigarette while waiting for the first Denver flight to arrive.

I had just flicked my butt at a skinny stop sign pole that we'd designated the target. I had just taken the lead, but Justin wasn't having any of it.

Howard was eating a sandwich and shaking his head.

"Just do it over, dude," he said.

"Fuck that. And lose my lead?" I bitched.

"Here comes Mathieu," Jax said.

Mathieu pulled up in front of us and looked at me.

"Hey girl, hey," he said.

"I got it," I said to him, knowing he would not have any idea what I was talking about.

"Okay." He shook his head. "You got it. Fine. Now, what did you get?"

He pulled his car up a little and put it in reverse to park. Backing up toward us, he parked perfectly in a space next to Justin's car. Getting slowly out of the car, he lit a cigarette and headed over to Jax's car to put his phone on the trunk, on top of a towel, to not scratch the coating. That's where all of our phones go when we're hanging out together in the lot.

Rule two is if you go over to look at your number, you don't touch anyone else's phone, but you call out their numbers on their screens. It took me a little bit to figure out everybody's phone.

I've got the method down pat now.

Rule one is, any phone not on the towel is expelled. That's a sign of major disrespect. No one is allowed to scratch another person's paint or car finish.

"Oh, God," Mathieu yelled, making his way toward us, smiling.

He has the tendency to do that when he's about to tell you something he thinks is really good. Or he responds to something he thinks you said was really good. Or when he's ready to tell you something.

Really, he says that a lot, but it's funny as hell and gets you fired up to tell a story or hear one.

"So, wait till you hear this one," he says. "You want to write a book, honey, put this in it."

Okay, I guess I will.

"So, I'm cruising over in St. Petersburg yesterday and I get a call from David. So, I'm like, okay."

"So, I'm like, okay" is another one of Mathieu's staple phrases. Almost every sentence he says leads up to something ending in, "So, I'm like, okay."

I loved it. Classic Mathieu, grade-A storyteller.

"So, yeah, so, okay, so I'm over in St. Petersburg and—

"This guy's food isn't bad." Justin came walking over with a plate from El Guido's food truck. He had a plate of what I describe as many different colors, but I think it was rice and beans, a few plantains, and what might have resembled chicken, but I wouldn't put $5 on that really being what it was.

"Really? That shit looks gross, dude, and fuck you, I hit it," I responded. "Okay, jackass?"

"Jackass?" Mathieu asked. "What did I walk into?"

Justin extended his middle finger in my direction and spooned a scoopful of rice into his mouth as he slowly worked his way toward food poisoning. Now *that* I would bet on.

"So, I'm over in St. Petersburg and I go over to this address," Mathieu continued. "And I pull up, and there's a man and a woman standing on opposite sides of the driveway and a cop is standing in the middle of the driveway next to his cop car, and I'm like ooookay."

One thing about Mathieu. You can tell how much drama is in the story by the length of the o's in 'okay.' 'Oooookay' is a really dramatic one.

"So, I pull up and the cop walks over to me and leans into the window of my car and says, 'Are you the rideshare driver?' And I'm like, 'Yeah? Look at my decal in the window, duhhh. What's the story?' I ask him. So he says, 'Okay, get this guy out of here in 10 minutes or I'm going to arrest him. I'm not dealing with this anymore and I've already been dealing with it too long.' Wow. So, I'm like, 'Oookay, I got this.'" Mathieu laughed hysterically.

"Ha, I got this. So, I get out of the car, put my hands on my hips, and scream at the top of my lungs, *'Nathan!',* and I'm like about five to seven feet away from him. I yell, 'Nathan!' and he looks at me and says, 'Yeah?' with a timid look on his face.

"I yell, 'Nathan, get the fuck in the car now or you are going to jail.'"

At this point, Mathieu couldn't stop laughing, so he took another drag of his cigarette.

The rest of us all lit cigarettes except for Jax, who doesn't smoke. And Howard, well, he had to bum one from me and then bum my lighter to light it.

"So, this guy looks at me, all panicked, and says, 'Well, help me get my shit in your car, then.' And I mean, shit, C.D.; he had a TV and a garbage bag full of clothes and two duffel bags, and I'm like, 'Wow, this is all of your belongings?' So, he starts hustling everything he has into my trunk—because you know me, I don't hustle for anything—and the backseat, and he jumps in the front. I'm headed back to the car and the cop looks at me and says, 'Damn, not bad.' And I say, 'That's right.'

"Next thing I know, we're cruising down 19 and I'm like, 'Okay, so do you want to tell me what all of that was about?' And the guy looks and me and C.D., I swear to God, he starts crying. I mean real tears and all and whimpering and he can't get out anything and he's like looking at me and he says, 'She wants a divorce and I didn't do anything and she's leaving me and I love her.'"

"And I'm like, 'That's it? Honey, you were ready to go to jail for all that?' 'He's like, 'Yeah.' So, I'm like, 'Okay. Where to now?' And he's like, 'I don't know. My mother's, I guess.' So I'm like, 'Fantastic' and I drive him all the way to his mom's so he can get out of the car and look at her and bawl some more in the parking lot before he looks at me and says, 'I'm okay. It's okay. Thank you.' And I'm like, 'Christ, just get your shit out of my car. You know, just get out, baby sweetheart.'"

Classic.

Totally funny Mathieu story and he always seems to have the police involved.

The funniest story I've ever heard him tell is the story from the time he was driving to perform a standup comedy act. He use to do it part-time in Lakeland, FL, and he truly is a funny man, so I can see why he would.

He was starving, go figure, and had just pulled over and bought some powdered donuts from a convenience store. As we always say to each other, if a fat guy is hungry, he's got to eat. So, in the midst of opening the donuts, he also turned on the radio and hit the AC fan knob by accident. The AC kicked in on high gear and blew the white powder from mini donuts all over his face and shirt, but more importantly at that time, he hit the steering wheel violently to try to turn the AC fan while he couldn't see from the powder being in his face and it caused the car to jerk a little to the left on the highway.

Lo and behold, a pair of red and blue lights turned on from behind his car and he started to pull over as the police followed him slowly to the breakdown lane. As the cop got out of the car and approached the window, Mathieu rolled the window down and immediately started laughing out of control and trying to explain that this was not what it looked like and that it was powdered donut residue. The cop took one look at the scene and started laughing as Mathieu explained the whole story.

"C.D., it looked like an eight-ball exploded on my face," he laughed.

I've heard that story about four or five times.

The story ends with Mathieu and the cop sitting for a few minutes, actually eating a donut together while Mathieu is trying to bang out the dusty white powder all over his upholstery, clothes, hair, and face.

Q number 21.

PAYPAL

I met Javon on a ride to a St. Petersburg hotel in the fall of 2017.

He flew in from Chicago, IL, and was coming to see his best buddy get married over the weekend. His buddy was a college pal he'd remained close with throughout the years, and now it was his buddy's turn to get married.

"I'm not getting married; we don't ever have to worry about me," Javon said with a smile. I wasn't worried.

Javon was a sports agent. He had, he claimed, about 15-20 professional athletes and college athletes under contract or signed to be under contract to go to the professional ranks someday.

He only dealt in football and basketball, yet it sounded like he had more football players under contract than hoops. He talked more and more about football and his liking for the game. You could see he was well-educated and studied the game a lot.

He flew in late on a Friday afternoon and I picked him up. He only had a duffle bag and a suit carrier.

"The wedding dress rehearsal is in 60 minutes," he said. "Fucking plane was delayed, shitload of people are out here, and the fucking terminal is loaded. It's fucking hot as hell down here. Tell you what, you get me to my hotel inside 60 minutes and I'll buy you a drink," he laughed.

"Well, it's only 5:30 p.m.," I explained, "so I can't accept the drink because I want to continue to work tonight, but I'll take the challenge. GPS says about 47 minutes."

"You are on, my man," Javon said.

Javon was a well-groomed African-American man. He was dressed in a suit and tie, looking like he could walk right into the rehearsal, anyway. He had a cell phone attached to his ear the entire time we were in the car. Given that he was an agent, I wasn't surprised.

He was dressed nice for travel, but you could still tell he had an image to uphold and it was important to him.

"I mean, who has their wedding in fucking Tampa during this heat and makes everyone fly there?" he asked.

Well, if the wedding is here and you don't live in this city, chances are, you'd have to fly here, no?

"Where's he from?" I asked.

"My buddy?"

"Yeah," I said.

"Chicago, South Side," he said with a dumb look on his face as if to say, *you should have already known the answer.*

It's always funny when people describe what part of the city they're from. People can't just be from New York; they have to be from Midtown or the Upper West Side. People can't be from Chicago; they have to be from the North Side or the South Side. People can't just be from Boston; they have to be from the Back Bay or the North End.

"And most of your other friends? Where are they from?" I ask.

"Chicago," he stares at me.

Man, now I'm seeing his point a little, but we have one important question left.

"Where is the bride from?" I hesitated.

"Chi-cag-o," he said. "Word."

I laughed. Okay, all Chicago people are present and accounted for in Florida this weekend, but obviously they didn't want to get married in

Chicago for some reason.

"So, I had to get on a plane, book a room, pack my shit, and come down here, when we could have just done this friggin' shit in Chicago."

The man had a point, I had to give him that.

"When you get close to the hotel, also, I need you to stop at like a store so I can get a few things," Javon rambled on. "No mouthwash because of airport security; ain't got no deodorant. Don't want to smell for my boy's wedding."

"Okay, I got you," I replied.

We talked a bit more during the trip. He seemed to be a cool guy. He explained how he went into meetings with sports agents, talked to them, and then went back to his clients. Being a sports fan, I was really into the conversation, but I took my occasional jab at Javon when we made a good stretch of time and it appeared more and more likely I was going to win our bet.

We pulled into a drugstore a few miles away from the hotel. Javon jumped out of the car in the parking lot.

"Do you need anything, man? Pack of smokes, soda, cold beer, anything?" he asked.

"No," I said. "I'm good."

I don't accept gifts from riders, ever. I don't know if it's because of me being paranoid, like Ms. Ava always tells me, or just my way of eliminating risks, but I just have never said yes to anyone buying me anything. I don't want my smokes messed with, my food spit in, or even my soda shaken so when I open it, it sprays all over me. I take that back; one time I accepted a fast food burger after a long ride. The rider handed me his credit card and I paid for it and watched it come from the worker. I don't want my stuff out of my sight. I have experienced stuff in management over the years, drivers putting laxatives in drinks, spitting in food, or even just breaking up a box of crackers to the point where it's a box of dust when you open it up. Most of the guys at the lot have accepted gifts. I'm sure it's 99 percent cool, it's just not my thing.

"Okay, I'll be back in few minutes," Javon said, walking into the store.

Then I got a text message.

Where are you? Justin asked.

St. Petersburg, I replied. *Headed back to TPA after this drop.*

Javon returned out a few minutes later, talking on his phone and seeming excited.

"Are you kidding? That's great news. He is really good," Javon said into the phone as he got back into the car. "He's an enforcer. Do you know what that means? That's a great signing."

I started to get excited; I don't know why, it had nothing to do with me, but I knew kind of what was going on, though not all the details. Then, Javon turned to me like I was one of the team members.

"Man, we just signed two wide receivers out of Indiana," he said. "Great day in the brotherhood and they are real good too, C.D., real good. I mean, this one guy glides when he runs, like no tomorrow, and the other is straight up. He has the height at 6'5", jukes and jives after he catches the rock, then flat to the house."

I was happy for him. I mean, imagine having someone with that type of talent choosing you to represent them for the rest of their life. It's an honor and privilege.

"Nice," I said. "Sounds great."

"Hell yeah, fuckin' nice," Javon said. He turned back to the phone. "That's great, Jonny. Oh man, I'm so excited. Damn, and the money those contracts are going to be worth? Hot damn."

"Me too. That means a good tip for the driver," I teased.

Javon looks at me. "Hell yeah, a fuckin' great tip. I'm going to tip you, cousin. You're my boy; you're a part of this shit now. I remember when. So, do you take credit cards?"

"No," I said.

"You don't have a Square?" Javon asked. The Square is a little gadget that you plug into your phone and use to swipe a credit card. I don't have one. A few of the guys have them at the lot, but they aren't enough of a huge difference for me to get one.

"Nope," I said.

"PayPal?" Javon asked.

"Nope," I said.

"Any credit means at all?" Javon asked.

"Nope," I said.

"I don't have any cash on me," Javon said. "The tip just turned ugly for the driver."

I stared again and really thought about this scenario.

We just left a store. If you were considering a tip, you had a chance to prepare.

We're going to a hotel. If you just did on the phone what you said you did, then go inside the hotel, hit up the ATM, and pay your newly-deemed member of the brotherhood.

If not, shut up about it and carry on.

Now I was turning the corner. *What a shittily prepared agent. I don't didn't know if I'd want him in charge of my finances or career. I'd never get paid, and I'd have to go to Chicago to get paid because the bastard thinks that it's the only city worthy of never leaving.*

Okay, that's extreme, but semi-truthful.

If I wanted to tip someone and couldn't because of a lack of funds, or more importantly, means, then when I got to where I was going, I would damn well make sure that my person was taken care of, whether or not it was going home and taking cash from my girl or kid, or hitting up an ATM machine. Not an empty swearing of solidarity from the king of brotherhood.

This is not how we're supposed to handle new memberships. Ehh, I was only in the brotherhood for another 2.4 miles until we reached the hotel. It was going to all be okay.

When I swung up in front of the hotel, Javon jumped out, grabbed his bag and suit, and stared at me for a few seconds.

"Man, you get to Chicago, I owe you a drink, at least," he said. If nothing else, he did; I'd won the bet at a robust 51 minutes, and on top of that, we'd stopped.

"Okay, next time I get there, I'll look you up," I said, even though I have vowed to not return to a cold weather climate again, and the Windy City doesn't sound warm at all.

"Better yet, here's my phone number; call me when you land. I got you," he said.

I won't hold my breath at that being the correct number at all or on you picking me up or being there for me.

Fair enough?

"Good luck to you, your clients, and the wedding this weekend, Javon," I said to him. "I hope you have a great time, and welcome to the Sunshine State."

"Right on, my man, right on." And away, Javon strutted into the hotel lobby. Empty promises and shattered dreams.

Q number 18.

RENT-A-FRIEND

Justin and I were sitting at the lot one day, in line for rides. It was a Sunday, summer afternoon, hot as hell. He and I were talking about some past rides to kill time. I was out of smokes. No Flick the Butt today, but I was enjoying a cold soda.

"I remember this dude from Seffner, man, he was a good guy, but wow," I said.

"Wow?" Justin asked.

"Yeah, he was a clingy dude; it was like he was my rent-a-friend for the day."

Justin laughed, adjusting his perpetual hat. It's usually a Denver hat because he's from the Colorado area. "I don't think I ever heard about that guy."

"Matt," I said. "I remember him like it was yesterday and this was about five or six months ago."

"What's the deal with Matt?" Justin asked, as he started to burn one.

"I'm just starting out for the day, over in Seffner. It's about 11:00 a.m. and I get a ping from Matt. Matt is a short, portly kid; he starts running to the car the second he sees me pull in the turnaround. He can't even keep his pants up. I should have taken him to a department store to buy him a belt. Anyway, he gets in the car and he's huffing and puffing like he just burned a full pack.

"'Okay,' he says, 'I need you to take me to my lawyer's and wait while I go in.'

"He assures me that it will only take a few minutes to sign a few documents and then he'll be out of there. 'Okay, I can do that,' I say.

"So, we pull out of his driveway and head toward the freeway to go to downtown Tampa, and on the way, he starts telling me his whole life story about how this is the fourth car accident he's been in and this one should be the most lucrative payout he'll ever receive."

"No shit?" Justin said.

"Yup. One head-on collision and three rear endings and today he's going to sign the paperwork to close this last accident. He's telling me that his right leg doesn't fully stretch out and more, and he has problems with his hips and all that, but he seems excited. So, we head downtown and I know by looking at the clock that we're going to be early, but I pull him in front of the building at about 12:35, after traffic. After telling me damn near all of the descriptive moments during the accidents, and what a great guy he is and how he never wishes harm on anybody, he recognizes the building we're at, like it's Santa's workshop.

"'Okay, park somewhere around here and I'll run up and see if he can sign these real quick and then we're out,' Matt says.

"'Okay, I'll wait,' I tell him. But before he can open the car door and step one foot out, his phone rings."

"Lawyer?" Justin asked.

"Yup," I said. "Well, now he's not going to be there until around two, so we should come back at 2:00 p.m. I'm like, 'Okay, I can drop you off and you call me when you're done; I'll come back and pick you up.' I was hoping to get rid of him and go make money somewhere else. He tells me that's not bad, but he really doesn't want to switch drivers because I'm a nice guy, and now he asks if I'm hungry."

"Which you always are," Justin said.

"Fuck you, but right," I reply. "So, I say to this kid, 'Where do you want to eat? I'll take you there so you can kill some time and we can come back.'

"'The burger joint,' he says, 'There's one right up on East Kennedy.'

"'Okay, let's go,' I say to him.

"So, I drive him there and he's like insistent that I come in and hang out with him and I'm now like, wow, this kid is like static cling. But, it's all good. I'll come in, have a soda, go back out, have a smoke, it will be 1:40 p.m., then we can turn around and head back and I can drop him, get our stuff signed, and shake this fucker."

"Yup," Justin said.

"So, we go in and he's eyeing me up and down already in line. 'What do you want to eat?' he says.

"'Oh, nothing, just a soda cup will be fine for me,' I say to him.

"'Come on, eat something,' he insists.

"'Nah, I'm good, but thanks,' I tell him.

"'Okay, I'll order for us," he says.

"He hands me the soda cup I requested and then seems pissed when I won't sit down at the table with him and watch him pound down a few cheeseburgers and fries.

"'Hey dude, we aren't friends,' I say to him. 'I don't even know you. I'm not a rent-a-friend, I'm a rideshare driver. I'll be outside. Having a fuckin' smoke.'"

"Haaaaaa!" Justin couldn't stop laughing.

"So, I'm out in the sun, standing in the parking lot, not killing cheeseburgers, and here he comes walking to me. 'Thanks man, for stopping; I was really hungry,' he says. 'I'm pretty full now.'

"'No problem. I'm so glad you're full,' I tell him. 'Okay, back to the lawyer?'

"'Yup,' he says. So, I pull back downtown and run up in front of the post office, where they have the standing area for trucks only and park right there while I watch his little chubby ass rumble across the street through a crosswalk and up into this really tall high-rise building. It's like 1:56 p.m. now. I'm thinking to myself, *it's all going to be good.* And I'm waiting and waiting and waiting. So, I fall asleep, because he doesn't come out for like ever."

"Oh shit," Justin says.

"Yeah, so next thing I know, I wake up to a loud obnoxious horn blowing. A big-ass postal truck is behind me, pissed off that I'm parked in front of his spot in a tow zone, and Matt is sitting next to me in the passenger seat, staring at me. Talk about having the creeps like in a movie. I look at the time and it's like 3:05 p.m.

"'Where the fuck have you been?' I ask.

"'Well, the guy wasn't there,' he says, 'So I waited a few minutes and then his receptionist asked me if I wanted lunch while I was waiting for him.'

"'You just ate, dude. I watched you pound down cheeseburgers not even an hour ago,' I say to him.

"'Yeah, I know, but,' he says, 'they were having tacos and they really sounded good and—'

"'Dude, you told me you were full when you walked out. Can we go, dude?' I ask.

"As the truck blows his horn again, I'm like WTF?

"'Yeah, we can go. I'm all done, all signed.'

"'Um, one question. How long have you been staring at me sleeping?' I ask.

"'15 minutes or somewhere around there,' he says.

"'Jesus, you're weird,' I say to him. 'Did it ever occur to you to maybe wake me?'

Justin was doubled over laughing at this point.

"'Okay, we are out of here. Let's go,' I say to Matt.

"As I pull away and jump on the highway, Matt is telling me that everything was done according to plan and that he should receive his check next week. So I say to him, 'How much?'

"He looks at me after a breath and says, 'Ohh, about $650,000 after fees.'

"'Dollars!!?' I scream at him.

"Shit!" Justin said.

"'Do you have a job, Matt?' I ask him.

"'Yeah, I work from home, doing internet work for a few websites,' he says.

"I'm staring at this dude like, wow, total amazement, and this is his fourth cash payout from car accidents. So, I get him back closer to his home; we're a few miles away and he starts requesting certain things again. By now, I have really had enough of this dude and his requests.

"'Hey, up on the left, about one mile is a gas station,' he says. 'If you stop, I can get my rare favorite bottled soda that you can't buy just anywhere.'

"*If* I stop? Does that mean he's requesting that I stop, or telling me to stop? I can tell you this, I couldn't give a shit about him in possession of his rare favorite bottled soda at this point, but why not? Why put an end to this ride just yet?

"At this point, I feel like I've been married to him for most of today, but there's a 50/50 shot that I might try to grab the favorite bottle of soda and hit him over the head with it when he's done drinking it. So as we pull up on this gas station, he looks at me and grins. Something is up.

"'I got seven extra bucks, too,' he says to me. 'I'll put that with the clerk inside and you can get some extra gas for your troubles of driving me around.'

"I'm thinking to myself, though, you got $650,000 today and who the hell else knows what you got from the other three settlements, plus you have an hourly job at home. I'm thinking I need to ask him if he needs a full-time driver." I started to laugh uncontrollably with Justin.

"So, I'm getting gas and Matt walks out, happy as a pig in shit over his plastic bag filled with three longneck bottles of soda and, of course, a lottery scratch ticket, which he will probably go home and scratch tonight and win $100,000."

"Right? Lucky bastard," Justin said.

"As we fire up the car and turned onto his street, I think to myself, this dude kind of grew on me. What a not-so-bad guy. I kind of like the guy in some way and feel sorry for him in others because he's just a nice kid who wants to fit in. When we get to his house, I tell him what a great adventure it was. Here it is, almost 5:30 p.m., and I spent damn near the whole day with him. He was genuinely a nice kid.

"'Thanks.' He smiles and looks at me as he prepares to exit the car.
"'Listen, I might need a ride tomorrow to do a few things and I have to go back to the lawyer on Friday. Do you want to give me a ride?'

"'No!' I say to him, as quick as I can; I mean, I could not have said it quicker. Nice kid, but I'm good. I don't need any more days like this, sharing time with him."

Justin laughed. "What's the target?" He held up his cigarette, smoked way down to the filter, ready to be flicked.

"The handicapped sign dead in front of us," I said. "$250 fine if you choke; feels like a strong westerly breeze, 10 knots, heavy humidity, and tough throw for the normal flicker. I'd play it left to right."

Justin reared back and pinched the butt. His arm motion followed through perfectly as he released the toss. Boom, he hit it with solid force, dead nuts in the middle of the sign to the point that the cigarette butt bounced backward off the sign.

Justin slowly walked away toward the bathroom, lifted his right hand, and pointed his forefinger in the air.

Q number 15.

SO HOW WOULD I FIX IT?

Dear CEO's of Ridesharing,

As I have been writing this collection of stories, and I'm sure even more now since you've been reading this, I've read in the news about where rideshare drivers across the country have been involved in situations where someone has been inappropriately touched, fondled, shot, hunted down, beaten up, and all different kinds of scenarios across the States that have had a negative effect toward all of us as a whole. It has kind of been a disgusting turn of events, and is somewhat embarrassing because when you're in the car with a rider, the first or second thing they bring up is usually, "Hey, did you hear about that guy or girl in Texas or Missouri who attacked someone during a ride?" And you're like, "Yep. It happens ohh too much."

So, how do we fix it, or for the sake of discussion, how would I fix it?

Well, there are a number of things to examine when you take a look at the overall problem. So, we can dissect and analyze them one by one.

Overall saturation of this job would be the first determining factor. Just because most everyone over the age of 21 can get a driver's license, that should not give them an automatic invite to be a rideshare driver. As mentioned in previous chapters, I've been in the transportation business for over 25 years. I've held special licenses, special access passes, and license endorsements to carry and haul a lot of specific and dangerous things. To hold those additives is considered a privilege, not a guarantee.

The first thing I think rideshare companies should do is get together with the federal government and decide on a special license or endorsement for this job, maybe call it a rideshare club membership. It should include a mandatory fingerprint for all applicants. This would weed out anyone who has a bad record or criminal history and should not be transporting people for an occupation. It would also create a revenue stream for the local city and states to have extra money. Some states I've lived in offer a chauffeur's endorsement; this could be considered similar to that.

I believe military people should be excluded from background checks as well. Most of our veterans have gone through extensive background checks already; there's no need to examine them again.

Any person interested in driving rideshare and who already carries a fingerprinted-issued document should be waived for just a nomination fee, not a reprint. In other words, if they have a current valid fingerprint on file with the federal government, maybe for a CDL license or TWIC port pass or an SIDA badge that shows up in a federal database, they should just be charged for the rideshare membership, not reprinted again. It will waste time and bog down the driver's license offices because every guy in the world already wants to be a rideshare driver, so adding that many people inside the offices on a daily basis will crowd them even more. Let's eliminate the ones we deem qualified from holding up our process.

The membership for ridesharing should be a one-year deal and an expiration date should be listed on their app so a rider can see that information. Every year, it should be renewed by every driver. This way, no one gets lost in the system during the new seven-year license renewal process. Nowadays, you can't shop at your favorite grocery store or go to a store in a mall without being asked if you have a rewards card or something of that nature. We should be able to create a hologram rideshare annual membership with a card that attaches to a keyring. Everyone should have a state-issued rideshare operation membership number, similar to a taxicab driver medallion number.

Let's charge a fee covering the process; we can pay the rideshare company a little bit for their business and charge a few extra dollars for a road and bridges state fund. If riders and drivers are going to use the roadways and bridges, then something monetary needs to be donated to these replacement projects. I would charge $75 per annual license. I wouldn't allow people to buy multiple-year memberships simply because they can afford it; we want to continuously check the backgrounds and mental state of these drivers.

Annual memberships would cost at most $75. I would ensure that $10 of the $75 per person was donated to a new government road and bridge repair fund committed to their respective state. $75 for an annual membership isn't an out-of-bounds number, considering we need offices to process this membership, a portion to go to the road and bridges act, the rideshare companies deserve a piece, and small amounts need to go to the cool laminated hologram card that can't be duplicated or passed on to an invalid driver.

Let's fix a problem somewhere else, if we're going to do this correctly.

Hazmat, buses, and other endorsements for transportation have a fee associated with them. Let's kill two birds with one stone, have a rideshare membership card, and fix a growing, potentially very dangerous country-wide issue, such as road and bridges repair in the U.S. Not only that, but this is going to weed out a lot of people who aren't serious about doing this for a profession.

The rideshare program in Tampa, for most of the drivers I talk to, is very saturated in the greater downtown area. Many people aren't making the money that they used to back when the program first started; for some people, this is a full-time job and they're very good at it. I don't think that just because an immigrant comes over from another country and doesn't have citizenship here, but can obtain a driver's license, that they should be able to slide in quickly without a fingerprint background check and be able to escort people around town. One major complaint I often hear from riders is that they can't relate to a rideshare driver or communicate with them because he or she doesn't speak English at all. That, my friends, is an issue, and for what it's worth, open your eyes and look around; the majority of problematic drivers are immigrants or people who don't look like they could ever pass a U.S. government background check. Say whatever you want, but just look around and examine the culprits before you say it.

Raise your hand if you have ever been in a taxi or rideshare car and have not been able to communicate with the driver because of his lack of English.

Now raise your hand if you felt 100 percent safe at that moment in time.

I'm not saying that people who don't speak English are not good people or that they don't belong in our country; most of them are very good people and our country is based on opportunity. That doesn't mean they should be shoved into a customer service role where they can't fulfill one of the major job requirements.

I would not run a freight company and put a customer service rep who can't relate to customers in charge of the phone to handle or input my orders.

I would not put a person in charge of a cash register or a clerk at a bank if they failed to demonstrate that they could count money.

Nor would I eat again at a restaurant where the cook couldn't cook an edible meal.

These people may be very nice even if they can't speak English, and they are very entitled to a job, just maybe not this one.

There are plenty of jobs in America where people don't have to communicate with others. If a customer asks, "Why are we taking this road to my home?" and the driver smiles at them because he doesn't understand what they're saying, is that not a red flag? Would you want your children or elderly parents or grandparents traveling alone in that car? And I understand that if you don't feel safe for that reason, there are other means of transportation and other opportunities, but I'm writing about this topic to fix my business, not offer alternative suggestions about how not to travel. I want people to rideshare. I want to make money and write stories about it.

In doing this profession for the last nine months, I have seen many people who can't drive, can't speak English, have vehicles in very bad shape, may not have quality insurance, and flat out just don't belong on the road. Headlights are out or there's bad body damage to their car. I can't tell you how many times my inner circle has commented on how, if you were paying premium money for a ride to your location, would you get into that car?

People are not going to pay $75 for a license to not take this job seriously. The license will more than weed out some of the issues these rideshare companies face. If not, I recommend other steps to help.

The next thing we need to do is have representation for companies at locations and be set up to do vehicle inspections. A vehicle inspection should be completed every 90 days and can be a quick inspection, such as headlights, rear and side lights, body damage, wipers, AC, and tires; an overall basic five- to seven-minute visual. If most companies require DOT inspections on vehicles every 90 days for tires and lights and extra stuff, then carrying people should be just as important as carrying cargo, and inspections should be done to normal cars that are in conjunction with this membership.

Charge a small amount for the inspection, make it quick, pair it up with local repair shops or have specific company locations or insurance agents do the inspection. If you want, donate a portion of this to the road and bridge repair association fund as well.

There are many drivers on the road doing this as a part-time job and I'm not saying that amount of people should be limited.

What I'm saying is that people need to go for an interview, get a thorough background check, be able to communicate with people, and have proper working equipment regulated and maintained to do this job.

Wouldn't you, as a rider, at least want the same background check done on a mall pizza clerk as on your driver? A piss test?

What if I told you that the checks were not even close to being the same? If words are just being taken for granted, nobody knows whether thorough background checks are being done on any drivers.

I know that I've had to sign to have a background check to be done on myself with every other job I've had.

But not ridesharing. I never signed a thing. A driver carrying produce or furniture has to go through the proper channels to drive, and we're not even mentioning random drug screens.

They tell you that you go through a comprehensive background check and then you get an approval. Never once have I ever heard of someone getting denied for rideshare background testing. Basically, if you have a regular license and insurance, you're qualified.

Raise your hand now if you're following what I'm saying.

So, let me continue to preach.

I also think a minimum number of points should be allowed on a rideshare driver's record.

One violation. Just one, which usually equates to three points.

If you've been pulled over and stopped by the police and have been given a citation more than once in the year, or manage to go above the three-point limit law, then your membership should be suspended from rideshare driving and you have to wait it out, just like any other DOT driver with a suspension or disqualification.

I could tell you how, in randomly talking to drivers in the lot, many drivers have at least had one drunk driving offense and one speeding ticket. Do you smell your rideshare driver's breath? Can you even tell if they are feeling good or happy if they've had a few odor-free drinks, such a vodka? Would you want to get into a car with them? Would you want to get into a car when the one ticket the driver had was a drunk driving offense? Ever? I think the program is wonderful for getting people who could potentially bring harm to others off the street by not letting them drink and drive, but have you ever thought of the reverse scenario?

This is one I've seen firsthand, and we could talk about it all day. I know some of my inner circle drives to make money, and sometimes it's not enough money to pay their bills or to live within their means, so they keep driving. Tired driving has always been an issue.

When is someone too tired to drive?

Should there be an hours' watch on your app when you get picked up by a driver that tells you how many consecutive hours they've driven and lets you decide of whether you want to ride with them or not?

The drivers can see how long they've been online in hourly amounts on their app. But the rider isn't given that information.

And what about the times that I talked about, like when Mathieu and I would shut off our apps and head back to the beach to get another ride early in the morning?

We're accumulating those hours in drive time, but that's not on our proverbial clock for online hours, even if you could see my time on your app from a rider's perspective.

If they're on their tenth or eleventh hour of driving, can you tell by looking at them?

Is their reaction time going to be as fresh as if it was their third or fourth hour of driving?

Shouldn't you be given that option to know and decide for yourself?

I firmly believe, although this can be a touchy subject for some people, that my rideshare driver shouldn't be handicapped or allowed a handicapped plate.

Every time I go to the airport to pick someone up, I get out of the car and handle bags for people. I'm in and out of the trunk; I open and shut doors for them. If we want to perform the best service and be participants in a great program, then we have to be 100 percent self-sufficient. If you can't perform the duties of the program, you probably shouldn't be involved. This is not about a nice-looking woman who's lazy and is trying to get people to do her job. This is about nice people who physically can't perform the job description. I handle 95 percent of bags going in and out of my trunk because I don't need someone throwing them in and scratching my paint or damaging my interior. Heck, ask Jax how that experience went for him.

I also think a sticker on a windshield should be a mandatory part of the car, not just a supposedly mandatory part of the car that never gets audited. A billion and two times, I have been told by a customer that the sticker in my windshield is was very helpful in identifying my car for their ride. Many drivers I see at the lot on a regular basis do not have a sticker. Some of that is to hide from the airport police when they come around to haggle or when a driver wants to park in a non-authorized rideshare area. Some of that is because people are too lazy to obtain one. Some of that is because people don't want to be identified as rideshare drivers while they're off-duty.

Put the sticker on the windshield when you're working. You're either all in or all out. It's a part of the uniform. You see golden arches every time you pull into that place to grab a hamburger and fries. It's part of the uniform. Every employee should be held to a high standard to complete the uniform. You're not asked to wear a uniform; we've seen you're not even held to standards to keep your car inspected, in good working order, or even clean. Put the sticker on the windshield.

From what I have seen, and this is just locally at my airport lot, I think there should be a representative from the company randomly rolling through the lot during heavily busy times to check credentials.

I'm not saying every day, but during heavy hours, I think if someone knocked on my window and said, "Hi, I'm here to check your membership and special hologram card, your sticker, and your other valid credentials," that would not be a bad thing. Alone on the road, it would be tough to flag down everyone, I certainly agree, but if we're talking about a mass quantity of 100-150 people at one time in an airport parking lot, a rep should be paid part-time hours to circle in and out of there, checking stuff on a regular basis.

These are just some of the things I've seen to make me wonder about how we could not only give riders a better experience, but make sure little things like their safety are better accounted for. Rideshare companies are each claiming an net annual worth of millions of dollars per year. The split that I'm having taken from me, per ride, which goes to the company to pay a high salary CEO or COO, is a hearty expense.

Is it going to stop all of the problems? No.

But if it stops one or two, have I really mentioned anything that sounds that ridiculous to put into action and see if it improves the quality?

Some of the greatest companies in the world live and die by quality assurance safety inspectors, and they aren't traveling with people and potentially endangering your life. I, most of the time, wonder how much better things would be if they just put one into the program.

Yours truly,

C.D.

Q number 12.

EVERETT

I was at the lot one Friday night, waiting for a call and shooting the breeze with Justin because we hadn't seen each other in a few days, and I got a call to pick up Marcus and take him to Tampa.

After talking with Marcus, I found that he was a nice young medical student finishing his residency and graduating from medical school that summer. He was living in Buffalo, NY, during the school year, and had recently had a job interview with a Tampa hospital and received an offer to work in the cardiomyopathy center. He was moving to Tampa and sounded pretty thrilled about it.

"No more winters for me, C.D.," he said to me. "I've graduated in two different ways, from the snow and cold to the warmth, and from a resident to a doctor."

"That's awesome," I replied. "I'm very happy for you." And I genuinely was, as he seemed like a good person.

We talked on the ride for a while, concentrating on medicine and cold weather, weather being something I know a little about, and about our kids and ridesharing. It was a solid talk, and we even shared a few laughs during the brutal Friday traffic. It wasn't until we were halfway there when I realized that his address was right around the corner from mine. It was getting close to 6:00 p.m. and we were approaching the gate to let Marcus in when I received a text from Ms. Ava.

I'll be leaving work around 7:30 p.m. What are your plans for dinner?

Normal distance time for her was about 45 minutes. That put her home around 8:45 p.m., giving me at least two hours, and she's never on time.

I could drive a little more since I was going to be alone if I went home, even though my general rule of thumb is if I get really close to the house, go home. So, on the app, there's a destination feature where you can tell the computer-generated system where you would like to head to if you receive a call for a ride, telling it to send you any rides going to that area. I naturally punched in destination TPA, figuring that if I could get a ride back to the airport, I could put the C.D. plan into effect and maybe take one there and pick up another. My own version of a two-for-one deal. Simple science. If not, and I just received a ride to the airport, I could at least go fuck around with Justin again and tell some lies and smoke one.

So, as I wished Marcus farewell and good luck while in front of his place, I drove to the nearby gas station to pick up my favorite cold soda drink and a package of cookies and set my destination app back to Tampa International Airport. Although 10 wings for $2.49 sounded attractive, not a normal decent wing cost of $0.50 a wing, so I have to wonder about the quality, I waited patiently as the clerk struggled to make change for a $10 bill, watching and waiting to pay for my cookies and drink. All of a sudden my app started lighting up and pinging while I was finishing re-counting the change the clerk had given me since I didn't think he was right. It's more of a beeping than a pinging, but for some reason, the inner circle group has always used the word ping.

I had a rider in waiting, and it was even closer to my house; it was from my actual apartment building address. That was weird. I don't interact with most of the people in my building; there really isn't any need to. I see a few of them now and then, carrying groceries upstairs or while I'm out at times, having a smoke, walking in from the car. I say, "Hey, how ya doin?" but never have any need for more than that except for Jimmy. Jimmy has a son around the age of Ms. Ava's daughter, and he has a dog. So, frequently, I see Jimmy out walking his dog or working on his car in his garage and say hello. Another person I see is my neighbor who lives on the second floor to the right of us. He's a younger kid, never got his name, but he's polite enough to wave every now and then, usually coming and going with his girlfriend or wife, whatever she is, who cares? He has jet-black hair, always uses his right hand to wave it back out of his eyes, seems to always dress nice, and again, he's polite. So I'm polite back, but I've never bothered to get his name. I have a few friends; I don't need any more. A friend at some point is usually in need, and a friend in need is a pest. I usually attract the biggest varmints in the world.

As I pulled around the corner to my building, wouldn't you know who was standing at the bottom of the stairs in front of his car, waving at me, but my neighbor, who we can now call Everett, because the app said so.

"What are you doing here, dude?" he asked as he opened the passenger door.

Well, I live here, but I drive rideshare, and he's fully aware I'm here to pick him up because my face is on his app as his driver and I have the sticker on my car. That probably gave it away that I was here for him, so really, why was he asking?

"Hey man, just out for a few bucks," I replied. "Ava is working late tonight and I figured I'd do a ride or two. I was down at the airport and it led me to over there on Palm Lane, so I figured I'd try to get one more ride and your call popped up on my screen. I figured I'd check it out."

"Cool. You don't mind going back downtown, do you?" he asked.

"No, not at all. I'll go wherever. No problems with that. What's up tonight?" I asked.

"Going downtown to have a few drinks. It's my birthday on Sunday, so my buddy is up from Miami for the weekend; figure we'd get lit up good and party."

"Right on. How old you going to be?" I asked.

"23," he replied. "Time to make some noise. And next weekend, Memorial Day, I'm headed down to Miami and we're going to do it up down there and reverse the tide."

Reverse the tide? Okay, I was older but not dead, yet I'd never heard that one before. But good for him, going out to tear up the town and have fun. Go for it, you champion.

"So, yeah, it's been a rough last week," he said to me.

Oh boy, here was the move for him to tell me all about his life, and I didn't want to hear any of it. I didn't want this. Some neighbor I saw from time to time, spilling his life issues on me, and I was trapped listening to them. I guessed at least I was getting paid to listen. You just knew it was coming, and he did not disappoint in description, content, or bulk.

"So, me and Cass are no longer. We broke up last week and I had to move her stuff out of the apartment with her dad, which was really emotional for me," he explained.

Why me? Who's Cass? Forget it, I don't care. Why me?

"Oh, your poodle?" I smirked. He had a dog that I had seen him walk from time to time. Maybe it was the dog? Whatever.

"Right?" he laughed. "I really thought she was the one. I mean, she was the perfect girlfriend."

Oh, your girlfriend. I was going to say her next.

Raise your hand if you thought it was the girlfriend. I'll give you a layup.

"I mean, for me, she has the perfect ass, tits, and face. I mean, I'll never get another girl that good-looking, and damn, she was fine," Everett said. "Too many emotional problems, though, with her menstrual cycle and all; hormones and shit."

My God.

"She's on that IUD thingy," he continued. "And her mother thought that would even out everything in her, but it made her worse and I don't know, maybe it helped, but I'm watching the game the other night on my phone, 'cause I love hockey, you know, and we're in the playoffs, and she's watching a movie, and now I'm in trouble for not watching the movie, which I've already seen, you know, bro?"

Are you going to take a breath in-between? I think to myself.

Why did I agree to this? I keep asking myself over and over in silence. *Why did I break my rule and not just go home?*

What makes me attracted to these situations like a magnet?

What on God's earth makes you think I want to know about your girl's menstrual cycle? I don't even care about my girl's menstrual cycle.

Now, the hockey playoffs? I get that. I mean, I'm not a big hockey fan, but if your team is in the playoffs, you've got to watch that. That's a guy rule, top 10 at that.

Bro? Were we bros now? Somehow I didn't think discussing his girlfriend's menstrual cycle elevated us to bro status.

"I mean, for me, perfect ass, tits, and face. I mean, I'll never get another girl that good-looking, and damn, she was fine," Everett repeated.

I've got to be honest; I'd never laid eyes on her. I was never close enough to do so. *So, if she has a nice ass and perfect features, well, dude, she's not yours anymore. It's completely irrelevant.*

"Yeah, bro, so, going for a few drinks tonight to take the edge off," he went on.

Again with the bro?

"And the funny part about it was, I sent the family a nice long text because I feel like their family, bro. I loved cooking spaghetti with her mother on Wednesdays and hanging out with her younger brother. I— here, I got it right here, read it. I wished her papa good luck on his future promotion and I know how hard it is to support the family and all ..." he went on and on.

Wait, dude, I'm driving, and I wouldn't want to read your ex-family's texts, even if I wasn't. It's none of my business and I don't care.

"So, whatever, that will make two exes that work on my floor at the insurance company, but I'll survive, you know, bro?"

That was funny, but I didn't want to engage in this biography anymore, though he kept trying to involve me further. Wisdom. My mother always told me, you don't shit where you eat. Everett needed more and more toilet paper, he was shitting so much.

"Great tits and ass, though," he said again.

"Wait, which ex?" I asked. I couldn't help myself, I had to.

"Exactly, bro. Good one."

Somehow, at that moment, I wished I was back to a normal regular rider who didn't talk a lot, just commented on the weather, and inquired about a good dinner restaurant to go to.

"So, I kicked her out and told her, get it together, like, I'm ready to settle down, and I want kids and I'm ready to have you as the one, and she needs to get it together," he said.

"Wait, *you* ended this?" I asked him. Son of a gun, he was the one to bring all this heartache upon his own self. He was crying heartache over this woman and he was the one to boot her in the ass out the door.

"Yeah, she needs to figure it out, and until then I'm going to the casino tonight with the $460 she just gave me; she owed me for a final bill and now I got the $460 and I'm ready to get ripe and I'm a monster at the casino, love the blackjack; I'm up $9,000 this year alone; a few drinks and some gambling and then down to Miami next weekend; we're ready to rock; I can just say that; I mean, I can find chicks, never had a problem with that, bro."

Here we went with the no breath again. This guy was going to die of oxygen deprivation if he didn't take a break from talking so much for so long. And what was it with people who get in my car and flash large amounts of money around? I had to ask.

"You have no issues getting chicks?" I asked him. "Really??" Okay, that was a jab, but I wanted to hear the answer. All five foot nothing, 130 pounds soaking wet of you, has zero problems getting babes? But you just said you'd never get a better-looking one than you just dumped, so why do you want to go out and find others?

"Bro, you can't find a better Oriental package than me. Good looks, the style, the looks; I mean, I have it all here," he replied.

"Got you," was all I could muster up. At this point, I was flustered and didn't have much to say, yet I was laughing so hard internally I didn't think that I could seriously look this guy in the face again. There wasn't enough wind in the car for both of us to speak and breathe.

We cruised closer and closer to his destination and I shook my head numerous times, wincing in pain and amazement over his story or maybe just the arrogance with which he told it.

As we pulled up in front of his watering hole for the start of his Friday evening, the car slowed down and he glanced over at me with the most serious look I had received in months.

"So, let me ask you something," he said, changing his tone dramatically.

Let me rehearse my potential answers really quickly in my head. Yes, you can tip; no, I won't be back to get you tonight; no, we aren't bros; yes, this car ride has been way too much for me, but no, I will try not to treat you any differently in the halls or the parking lot when I see you again.

"Umm, okay, go ahead," I said.

"So, do you really like chocolate that much?"

Wait, what? Did you just really ask me what I think you just did?

Everett stared at me slowly, waiting for an answer. He really did. He really did just ask that?

This is the time you have the right to say whatever you want, and you might run into that one motherfucker who doesn't like what you have to say and he reaches back and punches you right in the grill after you say it. He has the guts to ask that and has $460 in his pocket. At least, this would be the perfect time to have one less neighbor; I mean, I could dispose of his body easily and have almost $500 to do with as I please.

What a dick move to even ask that.

"I mean, I love chocolate cookies too, but bro, they will kill you. You can't eat too many of those," he said as he looked down at the cookies I'd bought earlier.

Oh, the cookies, I said to myself. *Sure, the cookies.*

What?

Did you think he meant something different?

Raise your hand if you thought he did.

Yes, I'm also raising my hand.

Q number 9.

SPECIAL ADULATION

So, we have told quite a few stories about people who have affected my life in a funny or not so funny way, but there are many that cannot make the book with their own full chapter. So, a few need to be recognized by being funny, mean, or just interesting people and get their credit by me writing a small tribute to them. After all, something is better than nothing, yes?

Take, for instance, my New York fish guys, Tommy and Tony. They came down to Clearwater Beach for a weekend to do some deep sea fishing and get away from the cold weather. I didn't drive them out to Clearwater, but I did drive them back to the airport. As I picked them up from their hotel on Sunday morning, they looked like two beaten dogs, red in the face from sunburns and arms and legs as tired as they could be.

They told me about fishing, what it took to find what they thought was the right boat and captain, and then they rented him for two days. They went out with Captain Jack and fished for eight hours the first day. After the first day, they were so tired, they just wanted to go eat, but with a twist—they were going to eat what they'd just caught. They'd caught over 40 pounds of fish and the captain wouldn't take it; he had plenty of his own. Jack told the boys about a couple of local restaurants that would cook their fish for them if they brought it in and asked. So, the boys, after asking Jack if he wanted it and being rejected, and asking if they could sell it on the open market and being denied that option, drove over to a local restaurant with all 40 pounds of fish.

"I knew when I walked in what I wanted to say to the guy," Tommy said.

"So, when he got close to me, I told him, 'Listen, we caught 40 pounds of fish today and we are freakin' dog-ass tired. So, here's what we want to do. Have the chef make five different types of fish with this and make the rest and give everyone in the house a bite so they can taste what we've done.'"

"So he did," Tony said. "He sent the waiter out with Cajun, blackened, sautéed, baked, and fried plates of fish. He brought us about 15 pounds. It was great. Then he blackened and fried the rest of it and the waiters served it to the other 65 people in the restaurant, including waitstaff and management. People were thanking us and shit. Buying us drinks. It was the best. What a good night. But I'm ready to go home," he laughed.

Tommy slipped me a $20 tip that morning in front of the terminal when I dropped them off.

"Best vacation I've ever had," he said, sporting an Armed Forces hat.

Speaking of which, I've had many veterans in my car along my last 1600 rides, and I know my guys at the lot have, too. One thing we always do when we find out is thank them for their service. Always thank them for their service. Many people have served our country and to pay them a small gratitude is a small way of acknowledgment.

I remember September 11, 2001 like it was yesterday.

I was working for the same small freight company back in Boston that had me traveling to the airport on a nightly basis. I was on the tarmac the morning of September 11, loading cargo freight into plane bellies at Logan International Airport in Boston There was a security guard we rolled up to every night to get access. Wayne was one of the coolest guys around. We used to stop and get him a cookie from the place we had dinner each night before going into the secured area to do our job.

I also remember the look on Wayne's face on September 17 when we arrived at the secured area, our first night allowed back into the loading area to get freight because, if you remember, planes were grounded for almost a week after. We had no cargo flying in or out for several days.

See, we had shown up to pick up morning freight that had touched down before all the flights had landed, and when we pulled up to the fence with Wayne's cookie in bag, a normally smiling Wayne was very stoic.

"IDs please?" Wayne said.

I had been to that gate every evening for many months and had brought him a cookie on most of those nights. We had talked at that gate about our wives, children someday, dreams and aspirations.

"Wayne, it's me," I said.

"IDs please," Wayne said. Now it appeared that Wayne was telling, not asking.

That day changed everything in our country as we knew it and I hope we never forget. I never miss a moment to thank a cop, firefighter, or a veteran of the armed forces. I was able to spend time in New York City just after September 11, having dinner and seeing a Broadway show. If you remember, at that time, the mayor was just pleading for people traffic, continuously saying that New York was open for business and to come down and spend money so the street vendors and local businesses could make money, so we went down and did our part. We spent half the night hugging, crying, and talking to law enforcement and firefighters and reading cards and letters at the original triage center. They are the true good guys who fight the evil forces and I shake their hands every time I see one.

Evil forces in Florida from July until about mid-October can be hurricanes. They're something we don't take lightly down here because of the potential severity behind them. I remember the bad one that came through in the fall of 2017. For Tampa, it wasn't as bad as the media made it out to be. I think we truly dodged a bullet. Some down in Miami and Key West took it much harder. Not to even mention the people in the U.S. Virgin Islands and Puerto Rico, who had a lot destroyed and thousands of man hours of rebuilding ahead of them.

I remember talking to Victor when the hurricane passed and we were able to have planes land in Tampa and transport riders again. The airport was only shut down for two days and Victor's flight came in from Dallas on Monday. Driving him over to Clearwater, I remember him talking about his dad.

"My dad lives in the U.S. Virgin Islands," he said. "I haven't had any contact with him in a week. I don't know when I will. The airport is destroyed, the runways are ruined, the towers are down, they have no phones, no cell service, and they're talking about weeks to months before it's repaired. On top of that, I don't even really know if he's alive or dead, to be honest."

Victor just stared out the window at the calm bay harbor as we crossed it to his destination, and I could only imagine what was going through his mind.

All I wanted to do was hug that man.

Another guy I wanted to hug was 24-year-old Brad. Brad was completely blind. I picked him up from a school over in St. Petersburg and, as I pulled around the campus looking for him, my phone rang and Brad gave me instructions to his location. I had never been on the campus before, he had never even seen the campus before, and yet he guided me around like he had been looking at it all of his life.

While I drove him to his apartment, Brad explained to me that he had contracted a serious disease when he was a baby and his eyes had to be removed at the age of five. He had lived most of his life in Florida and actually attended the college I picked him up at that day. He was a double major and was working on his architectural master's degree.

"I want to build the tallest buildings in the world," he told me as he sat in my front seat. He had the greatest attitude in the entire world and I'm grateful for getting to spend 27 minutes with him. After pulling into a parking spot in front of his apartment, he asked me how many spaces we were from the handicap ramp if I counted from the right. After telling him two, he jumped out of the car like he was fired out of a cannon.

"I'm going inside to make a grilled cheese," he said.

"No shit?" I said.

"No shit," he said with a smile.

I ended our ride with, "Brad, you're a great young man and I wish you all the luck in the world."

"Up high, my guy," he said, as he extended his hand to high five me.

What a great spirit.

Actually, he's not the only blind passenger I've ever had. I also had Greg.

Greg was going from a bus terminal to a train station to go back to Ohio. I picked him up outside the bus depot and a woman walked him over to my car.

Greg was much more timid then Brad and a little older, but a solid figure despite his handicap.

Greg talked to me during the 12-minute ride to the train depot, mainly about his plan for me to park the car and walk him inside the depot to a teller so he could purchase his ticket. Greg went over that plan about 450 times in 12 minutes and, as I pulled the car up in front of the depot, I could tell something was not right from the start. Quite a few people were standing outside the building. I looked at Greg and told him what was going on, and he kind of shit his pants a little bit.

I don't think he was the go-getter that Brad was.

"Can you walk me up to the door?" Greg asked.

"Sure, I will," I said to him. "You want me to wait until they open?"

"Nah," he said. "I'm in front of the door to the ticket depot?"

"Yep."

"Okay, I'll just walk up the two small stairs here and in the doors," he said. "I'll make it. And they'll help me move on further."

"Okay, buddy."

"Hey, five stars for you, C.D.; you're the best." Greg said as I walked away from him back to my car. Can't help but say I was a little worried about him.

I would have liked to spend more time with Brad and Greg; they were both very good people.

People I don't want to spend much time with at all, if any, are airport traffic cops.

Most of them are grouchy and a downright pain in the ass, and none of them have a cohesive plan of action. There was one night where I pulled up to the blue terminal on consecutive rides. The first time I pulled in, I was going to the airline furthest down the aisle. So, like a highway plan, I sped up in the left-hand lane and went two thirds of the way down the terminal to pull up and cut in over to the right in front of my people. One of the main reasons I chose to do that was because I had a traffic cop standing in front of me, asking me where I was going.

"Down to the last airline," I said.

"Okay," he said, "Go left, head down, cut in before the last airline, and pick up your people."

"Thanks, man," I said to the cop. At least he was thinking. This area was swamped, so jump in the left and cruise down and cut in.

But the next time I came around the corner and the picture painted an almost exact scenario, I got to the last airline and a woman traffic cop started screaming at me.

"I ought to give you a ticket for that shit," she said.

"Excuse me?" I replied. "I know you aren't talking to me that way."

"Yes, I am. Do you want a ticket for cutting in like that?" she asked. "The next time you do that, I'll ban you from picking up here."

"Why are most of you ignorant and combatant?" I asked. "You make things so much harder for us and you're so confrontational. Are you just pissed because they won't let you carry a gun? Maybe you're pissed because if you don't get to carry a gun, you're not a real cop? You're like one step above a rental cop? To make things worse, your guy down at the front told me it was okay to cruise down here and cut in."

What a bitch.

I see that woman from time to time in the terminals. We don't have much to say to each other. It's my intent to never talk to her again. It won't be that hard.

But I like to get rowdy from time to time. Who doesn't?

Q number 6.

GO ON IN?

So, there are times in your life when you make decisions and you wonder whether you made the right one or not.

Whether it's a decision that could affect your life, or a meaningless one that no one may know about, such as how to drink your scrumptious freshly brewed cup that day, it's a decision. It can be hard or easy. It's all up to you to make, well, the right decision. Or sometimes, you make the wrong one and you pay for it dearly.

That brings us to Krystal.

I was at the cell lot one Friday night, about 11 p.m. I had made a good night in money and now greed had set in, so I thought I would get one more ride and head home. That last ride is the one that I always hope will pay for my full tank of gas at the end of the night for the next day. Ava was waiting for me to come home safe and get to bed, and we were traveling to Orlando early the next morning to spend the weekend together.

I got a ping from Krystal at the blue terminal. So, I messaged her like I've done a thousand times for others, and headed up over the bridge, under the people tram, past long-term parking, and toward the terminal signs to pick her up. It really wasn't a feeling like any other, yet little did I know that it was going to be a very challenging night.

As I pulled around the bend to the terminal and passed the first group of people, I got a text back from Krystal. It read: *I'm all the way at the end, pink hair and a purple boa.*

A purple boa? That one shouldn't be too hard to find. I had to see this one. Pink hair, in itself, is not a thing you see walking around the streets these days. Every once and a while you do, but it's not common. Now, a purple boa just had excitement written all over it, or complete oddness, one of the two. Like I said, this story I needed to see and hear about.

At the end of the terminal, I saw Krystal, and she wasn't lying. In a sea of people waiting to be picked up, she was a pretty attractive, tall, thickly-built woman sporting pink hair, a purple boa, and an outfit of a white top and a pair of black leggings. This was a rather easy one to point out, given all of the regular stuff I see at the terminal. I'm used to seeing blue jeans and black shirts, maybe gray or brown hair; quite frankly, all the people blend together when you've done a bunch of rides in one day and are trying to fish the last one out of a crowd late at night.

The normal things. But not Krystal.

Power-pink hair and a 10-foot purple boa.

Nice. Get on in. Let's do this.

I popped out of the car with extra pep in my step, wanting to hear the story. It was later than usual, and I was trying to keep myself awake for this last ride. I greeted her with a smile as she looked up at me, rolling two heavy-weighted striped bags in my direction. You could almost hear the wheels screaming as they rolled. Nonetheless, I picked them up and placed them in the trunk and headed back around to my door. When I heard the rear door shut, it was just like any other ride. And why shouldn't it have been? Her hair color wasn't going to change that.

"Are you all set?" I asked.

"Yes, I'm good," she replied in a low, quiet voice. That set the mood and tone. Very nice, sexy voice.

Away I slowly pulled from the terminal, headed under the final stretch of lights past runway 19R into the night as I swiped the screen and found out we were headed to St. Petersburg. Given what I'd just picked up, and in an effort to keep myself awake, I had to ask a few questions.

My radio was playing softly, but I turned it down another level to prepare myself for the barrage of questions I had. I was lining all of them up in my head when she beat me to the punch.

"So, have you been doing this long?" she asked.

"About nine months," I said.

"Any crazy stuff happen to you?"

"No, usually pretty boring," I said. What I could have told her then is what we know now. At least 200 pages worth of a book had happened to me.

"Tonight won't be boring," I thought I heard her say. I almost swear on my life and children that's what came out of her mouth. But I didn't reply or ask her to repeat; I just smiled in the rearview mirror at her and headed over the bridge to make our trip.

"So, I gotta ask," I said. "What's with the boa?"

"Okay, so, I was out in LA this week at a conference," she said.

Okay. Story over, this is boring. She's a young hippie type who wanted to be important in LA and she decided to wear her craziness home and blah blah.

"Cool. L.A. is nice," I said. "What were you doing out there? Visiting family? Friends? Movie shoot?" Hey, you never know.

"No; okay, so I was at the national BDSM convention," she said.

Raise your hand for the final time tonight if you know the definition of that. Most ladies should be raising their hands due to a certain movie that swept the nation and explained this cultural phenomenon.

I don't know why I know that one or how. Well, I do know why and how, because I used to run a pair of video stores for my father when I was much younger and I used to put the movie titles into the computer system. I controlled all of the inventory and we frequently had pornographic titles in our inventory because the local crazies loved to rent them. Okay, I'm guilty. I've seen a few hundred boxes, putting barcodes on them, and I may have read a title and blurb on the back, or two.

BDSM is an acronym for sexual erotic practices. It involves bondage, discipline, dominance, submission, sadomasochism, and others, to say the least. More and more, over a period of time, it has grown into a culture, not so much a selective practice anymore.

"I'm a professional dominatrix," she said with confidence and a smile, staring out the window.

I nodded and stared ahead at the windshield for a while, trying to comprehend.

Dead silence loomed through the car for a good five minutes. Five minutes is a very long time when you aren't talking and you're only thinking; it seemed like hours.

"How old are you?" I asked. It was the only thing that came into my head.

"23. Almost 24," she said.

Then the next thing that immediately came through my mind at my age of 46 was, *nobody in any profession is a professional at the age of 23. Oh, and I don't care if you're almost 24; you're 23.*

Nice. Cool ride. Okay, where do we go from here?

There were some things that just didn't strike me and give me that wanting feeling. Looking at her legs was one of them, or her body. I didn't care; I wasn't interested. I don't know if it was the age difference or the nature of the beast or the chances she had probably been with more men at 23.5 then I had been with women at 46. And again, I have Ava at home. After recently divorcing a few years ago, I'm ready to start spending my life with her.

I just wasn't interested in Krystal, even though she was attractive.

But the lifestyle and unknown potential that rattled through my head, revolving around the topic of BDSM, was limitless. What was it like to be blindfolded, tied down, whipped, or anything along those lines?

Okay. I was interested, yet it really didn't have anything to do with what she looked like. It was more of the lifestyle she led and claimed she was a professional at. Maybe she had mastered it. She could have been studying the topic for years.

I go to baseball games and sporting events and call myself a fan. I watch them on TV and constantly read about them. I study the game like an art. I'm aware of the history, the rules, and all that goes on with a great game. I would definitely call myself a professional sports fan. I mean, come on, I understood that 25 wins in 24 games was impossible.

Krystal walked around in public, hiding a secret life of punishing people, sexually embarrassing them, or granting them wishes for whatever they craved behind closed doors. She fulfilled the fantasies of men who coughed up serious amounts of cash to have wild and crazy stuff performed on them and in front of them. She attended conferences and gatherings about this topic as easily as I sit and eat peanuts, drink beer, and keep the book.

She edged baseball out on this comparison with the overwhelming rarity factor. Simply put, I do mine in public and her profession was in private, so it's hard to get an accurate count of how many followers of the culture there are. They don't make a hat with a BDSM logo on it that people walk around proudly wearing. Well, maybe they do, but it's much easier to spot hats with the more identifiable red B on them, like I wear.

They have a safe word; we run home, hoping to be safe. Nothing alike. Two totally different games of pitching and catching, never mind rounding the bases. Okay, that's enough baseball-related euphemisms.

Maybe it's because I don't know much about it. It's the unknown to me, but it's a very interesting topic. Maybe because there aren't any rules or boundaries and my baseball rules are no more than four balls, three strikes, and in the seats is out of play.

I don't know.

"C.D.?" she said.

"Yeah?"

"You okay?" she asked.

My mind was going a little crazy right now with curiosity.

"No, I'm good, yeah, fine," I responded, trying to play it off the best I could. "So, it must have been wild out there in L.A., huh?"

"Yes and no," she said. "I actually went out there with a client who flew me out there. He's one of my big clients. A real high roller."

"Clients?" I said.

"Yeah," she said. "I have two to three pretty good clients who like to go to shows with me and I set stuff up for them from time to time. They fly me out and rent rooms for us to stay in and then they give me certain requests and I honor them. This guy this past week wanted to be tied up and in a room with four women, so I coordinated the women and we pretty much beat his ass and tormented him from one side of the room to the other all night long. He loved it, but of course he would; he asked for it."

Damn, that's a lifestyle, all right.

"I came home a day early because he and I had a fight about it," she continued. "As of Wednesday morning, I had not set up his request, so he got angry and thought I wasn't going to come through. I woke up to him screaming and yelling and him asking me what he was paying me for. So, I made a few calls and set up what he wanted and after we beat his ass Wednesday night, I asked him to move my plane ticket up to Friday. I wasn't taking his shit. I produced, and he treated me like shit. Oh sure, afterward he was apologetic, but I felt like it was too late. So, now I'm home."

So, through the dark we headed to her complex and, upon pulling in, you could tell that she was a fan favorite. The guard at the security shack recognized her and smiled as we pulled in, opening the gate for us without even needing to see her ID.

Krystal was friendly to all and acted like most normal people who were just looking for a ride home from the airport. The only problem was, she was also a woman with a secret, dark craving for a lifestyle that is very interesting. They always say the quiet ones are the freaks.

Heading down a dark alleyway at about 11:45 p.m., we pulled closer to her drop-off point.

"It's the third one on the right," she said as I approached, going over the second speed bump.

God, I hate those things, by the way. Nothing good comes from speed bumps, especially the wear and tear on my car.

As I swung around and parked off to the side of her staircase, I turned the car off and pulled on the handle to open the door when she leaned up front a little.

"Okay, so, I have a proposition for you," she whispered.

OMG, here we go. I mean, this is the kind of stuff you read about in books.

LOL. Sorry. But it is.

I took a long, deep breath, turning my eyes to the sky and waiting for what I thought was going to be a—well, I didn't know what was coming, but I was pretty sure I knew what was coming.

"This is the part of the car ride I was waiting for," I said, with a smug tone, yet really with my heart was in my throat the entire time.

"C.D.?" she said.

"Yes?" I answered.

"Okay, so, I have two bags in the trunk. You know that from helping me earlier, and one of them is very heavy. I live on the third floor, so I was wondering, I mean, I'll totally tip you, if you'd carry the heavy one upstairs to my floor?"

"Oh sure, of course," I said.

Come on, what did you think she was going to say? Come on in and let's hang out in my room so I can mercifully beat and whip you and have sex with you, since you seem so interested in my lifestyle?

And I have the beautiful Ms. Ava and nothing was going to screw that up for us.

Nothing.

No choke collar, wrist cuffs, sex swing, or any other stuff in this so-called profession could she approach me with to change my mind. Ava and I are passing our two-year anniversary point. Things are awesome for us. We've plotted out a future together.

"Sure," I said with a sigh of relief. "I can carry that up for you." To be honest, I had no clue what I would have said or done had she suggested something different.

"Bonus," she added, "I might even have a treat for you."

Wait, what?

The first floor was okay. Second floor was annoying. And the third floor, I was getting darn tired. This bag was heavy. She wasn't joking and I was pretty much done with carrying it.

"My money is inside," Krystal said. "Just put the bag over there on the sofa," as she unlocked the door and we entered her apartment.

At the entry, her apartment was pretty normal. Two bedrooms, she claimed, about 1200 sq. ft. A little bit of color on the wall, and neutral-tinted furniture. I noticed the big tan couch over in the corner, so I approached it to place the bag on top of it.

"What's in this thing, concrete?" I asked.

"Just some of my stuff that I travel with," she said, as she entered a doorway and turned on a bright maroon light.

"How much was the fare, so I know what to tip you?" she asked from the other room.

"$17.21," I said, waiting patiently.

"Okay, I have change around here somewhere. Fuck, I can't find it," she said, sounding disturbed.

At that time, I received a text from Ms. Ava. *Hey honey, waiting for you. Be safe coming home. I love you.*

I needed to wrap this up and get out of here. I was wasting time and was never going to get a decent tip. I think it was just a ploy to get me to carry up her 2000-pound bag. *Okay, you got it. It's up here, I'm out of here.*

"If you want water or something, I know you've been working all night. If you're thirsty, just grab something out of the fridge, it's cool," Krystal said.

"I think I'm good," I responded, "I had my coffee earlier on and I'm due for another coffee on the way home."

You all know by now how I feel about my coffee.

"Yeah, I don't do coffee; I don't like coffee. Sorry I can't offer you one, but I think I got water and something else in the fridge. Sprite, maybe?"

Let's just hope she didn't know Manny.

Doesn't like coffee? What type of girl did I bring home? And what the hell is taking so long for a tip? Did she get lost in her room looking for money?

Let's do it. Let's peer our head through the doorway and just tell her, hey, it's okay if you don't tip; I'm cool. A hot cup of hazelnut dark roast sounded good, anyway. It was just one bag. No biggie.

As I stuck my head through the door, I turned to the left and noticed that it was Krystal's bedroom. Maroon light shining, looked like a queen or king bed in the corner, pressed sheets—very clean, hardwood floors, and, as my eyes rose, I was shocked.

"Ready for your tip?" she asked.

Krystal was kneeling on the bed in a white lingerie outfit, a blindfold in her left hand and a flogger in her right hand. A pair of steel handcuffs lay on her pillows. There were a few braces bolted to the ceiling and dangling down, hovering just above bed level.

"Come in, C.D," Krystal said. "Come in and lay down. Money is overrated. Let me tip you."

WTF. I can't do this shit.

Ava and I are too involved. Plus, I love her and we're headed to happiness. I mean, Ms. Ava is one of the few you find in a lifetime to spend your life with. Smart, beautiful, sexy, and also very into me.

Krystal extended her left hand with the blindfold.

"Just put it on and I will guide you," she said. "I will introduce you. I could tell you had a serious interest in the BDSM lifestyle when we were talking in the car. I could tell when we walked into my apartment that you have an interest. I will hold your hand through it all and show you what this is all about."

She wasn't wrong, but to what level was my interest?

My curiosity was crazy, I'll admit that. My mind was going 100 mph as she was talking about the unknown to me, which was the very well-known to her.

Only problem was, she wanted to make it well-known to me.

"Just put this on and allow yourself to relax," Krystal said. "You'll be fine. Nothing will be said; no one will know anything, and you can come back at any time if you desire. That's it, C.D., baby steps. Come on in and sit down right here and ..."

Krystal got up off the bed and started to circle around to my side of the room.

She walked with a confidence that oozed. I was just hoping that she wasn't going to get to me and make anything else ooze on my body.

"C.D., come closer," Krystal said with conviction. "Come to me. It's quite okay. You need to release yourself and let your mind and inhibitions run ..."

Ping, ping.

Red Terminal, Walter is 3.9 miles away. My thumbs are getting cramps. It's about time I got a call; time to start my day. Finally, let's go up to the terminal and get Walter, make some money, maybe have more information to tell another story.

I'll be back again, I hope. If I am, we can raise our hands again and tell a few more.

Thank you for reading and listening. BBFN.

ABOUT THE AUTHOR

R.C. Otovic was born in Danvers, MA in September 1971.

He grew up in West Newbury, MA and graduated from Pentucket High School in 1989.

He majored in Business Management at CCSU in Connecticut in 1989/90, where he was a sports editor for the school newspaper, *The Central Recorder,* and did some freelance work for the *Hartford Courant*. He also hosted a sports radio show on WFCS in New Britain, CT.

R.C. majored in journalism, accepting a full scholarship at NECC in Haverhill, MA, from 1991 to 1994, holding the titles of sports editor and managing editor with the school newspaper, *The NECC Observer*. During that time, he helped guide his staff to two consecutive National Collegiate Pacemaker awards, an AP Best of Show award in Los Angeles, CA and was offered internships with the *Boston Herald* and *Lawrence Eagle Tribune*.

After that, he worked in the transportation scene for 25 years, driving and managing in different fleet services.

He currently resides in New Tampa Palms, FL, with his girlfriend Kim, her daughter, and his two boys. He currently manages a fleet delivery service, works part time as a rideshare driver, and writes on the side. During his free time, he enjoys a fresh cigar at Nicahabana Cigars in Ybor City, FL, or relaxing with a glass of wine with Kim.

RICHTER
PUBLISHING

www.ingramcontent.com/pod-product-compliance
Lightning Source LLC
Chambersburg PA
CBHW072223270326
41930CB00010B/1977